Graphics from
The New Print Shop

The ABC's of
The New Print Shop

The ABC's of
The New Print Shop®

Vivian Dubrovin

SYBEX® San Francisco • Paris • Düsseldorf • Soest

Acquisitions Editor: Dianne King
Developmental Editor: Vince Leone
Copy Editor: Ami Knox
Technical Editor: Linwood P. Beacom
Word Processors: Scott Campbell and Deborah Maizels
Book Designer: Jeffrey James Giese
Chapter Art and Layout: Suzanne Albertson
Screen Graphics: Delia Brown
Desktop Publishing Operator: Daniel A. Brodnitz
Proofreader: M. D. Barrera
Indexer: Julie Kawabata
Cover Designer: Thomas Ingalls + Associates
Cover Photographer: Michael Lamotte

To my husband Kenneth P. Dubrovin, with thanks for his support and encouragement

Acknowledgments

I would like to thank Ruth Thomas for the use of her IBM PS/2 Model 25 computer, IBM Proprinter II, and her constant encouragement.

I'd also like to thank Reverend Lynn Evans for his help in converting disks and researching large signs.

Thanks to Brøderbund for designing a fine product to work with and for supplying the copies of the software that I needed.

And many, many thanks to the people at SYBEX: to acquisitions editor Dianne King for suggesting the project, to developmental editor Vince Leone for his patience and understanding, to copy editor Ami Knox, and to the entire production staff for their support.

Contents at a Glance

Table of Contents

6   *Using the Name File*   *167*

Introduction

The New Print Shop is a creative tool that anyone can use to design exciting products, such as greeting cards, signs, banners, letterheads, and calendars.

The original Print Shop was one of the most popular pieces of software ever created. It introduced computer operators to the idea of creating and printing such products as greeting cards and signs on their computers.

The New Print Shop now goes beyond the original version by adding new features and additional creative opportunities.

What This Book Is About

The ABC's of The New Print Shop picks up where the documentation for The New Print Shop stops. It provides step-by-step instructions and samples for using the projects and features, and presents design ideas that will help you explore all of the possibilities of this new program.

Chapters 1 through 5 cover the five projects in *The New Print Shop*: Greeting Card, Sign or Poster, Letterhead, Banner, and Calendar. Each of these chapters presents an overview of what the project can do, step-by-step lessons to create sample products, and mini-lessons to explore additional features.

Chapters 6 through 9 explore the capabilities of some of the program's special features—the Name File, Quick Print, the Graphic Editor, and the Customize feature.

Chapter 10 discusses where to find extra borders, graphics, and fonts to use in your designs.

Chapters 11 through 13 show how to integrate the projects to create materials for particular activities, such as seminars, conferences, dinners, sales, and bazaars.

Chapter 14 presents extra printing and photocopying tips.

Who Should Read This Book

Anyone who is using The New Print Shop for the first time and wants to learn how to use some or all of the projects and features will find the instructions they need in this book.

Users of the original Print Shop who want to learn about the new possibilities in this version can read about them here.

Everyone who wants ideas for creating products with The New Print Shop for their businesses, organizations, or church groups will find suggestions in this book.

How to Use This Book

You do not need to read this book from the first page to the last. You can select the project or feature you want to learn about and read the corresponding chapter first. For example, if you want to make a sign, read Chapter 2, "Making Signs and Posters."

If you are directing a conference, seminar, or workshop or are in charge of a dinner, sale, or bazaar, you may want to start with Chapters 11, 12, and 13 for some ideas.

You may discover, however, that there are so many ideas sprinkled throughout the book, you will want to read it from cover to cover so you don't miss anything.

Hardware Requirements

The ABC's of The New Print Shop was written for IBM PCs and PC compatibles. The New Print Shop is available in both 5-¼ inches or 3-½ inches disks. It requires MS-DOS 2.1 or higher and 512K of memory.

You should have a graphics card and monitor and will need a printer to print the products. A mouse is also very handy, but not necessary.

If you plan on printing in color, you will need a hard disk, 640K memory, a color graphics card, a printer capable of color printing, and a multicolor ribbon.

You will also need formatted disks for storing your creations. The program does not allow you to format a disk from within the program as the original Print Shop did.

Appendix A at the end of this book gives more information on how to get started with The New Print Shop on your computer.

A Look at the New Print Shop

There are five main projects in The New Print Shop:

The Greeting Card project allows you to produce a side-fold or top-fold card and print cards in different sizes. You can print a ready-made card, design your own card, or reprint one you have previously created and saved.

The Sign or Poster project allows you to create a sign which can be printed on a single page or across several pages. You can use one of the full page designs that comes with the program or create your own.

The Letterhead project also contains ready-made panels but allows you many choices in creating your own unique layouts.

In the Banner project, you can create a vertical or horizontal banner with graphics on either end and border designs. You can use one or two lines of type and print it across the width of either a single page or two pages.

The Calendar project allows you to design yearly, monthly, weekly, or daily calendars and print them in various sizes.

The New Print Shop also has many special features:

With Quick Print you can print out a single graphic or line of text to use somewhere else, such as on a bulletin board or in a newsletter.

The Graphic Editor allows you to create a new graphic or bring a picture onto the screen and change it.

The new Customize feature allows you to make many changes to your graphics, fonts, and layouts.

The greatest strength of The New Print Shop is the ability to make changes and to preview those changes before you print your products. You can now change your design at any stage of the creation process. You can modify your layouts, graphics, fonts, and borders. You can even bring old creations back on screen and make adjustments before printing them again. You can use more than one graphic per page, move graphics anywhere on the page, and shrink, enlarge, or flip graphics. You can change fonts and font sizes on any line.

Using The New Print Shop can be fun, easy, and rewarding! But to discover just how much fun it is, you must turn on your computer, load The New Print Shop, open this book, and begin.

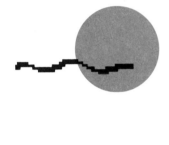

1 Creating Your Own Greeting Cards

The New Print Shop

MAIN MENU

Greeting Card
Sign or Poster
Letterhead
Banner

The New Print Shop gives you the ability to create a wide variety of cards and invitations with ease. You can choose a ready-made card (and customize it for your own use) from one of twelve designs included in the program. Or design your own card by selecting from an assortment of borders, typefaces, and high-resolution pictures.

The New Print Shop also allows you to

- Assemble borders, words, and pictures on both the front and inside of the card

- Create either a side-fold card or a top-fold card

- Place a one-line credit on the back of the side-fold card

- Print your card in six different sizes, from the normal 4¼-by-5½-inch size to a tiny 2-inch gift enclosure size

While you are designing your card, The New Print Shop lets you see your creation in the PREVIEW box on the right side of your screen. Afterwards, you can store your creation on a separate disk to use another time. You can always modify it before printing it again.

Because the Greeting Card project of The New Print Shop offers so many options, the best way to understand this part of the program is to create a few cards. In the following sections, you will learn to

- Load and customize a ready-made card

- Design your own card

- Print out a gift- or enclosure-size card

Later in the chapter, you will have the opportunity to explore other Greeting Card options.

Using a Ready-Made Card

Let's begin with the Anniversary card, a ready-made card that comes with The New Print Shop. This will let you see some of the things that the Greeting Card project can do and introduce you to the MAIN MENU and the printing options.

How to Use the MAIN MENU

Before you can use The New Print Shop, you must install it on your computer. (See Appendix A for installation instructions.) Once installed, you can start up the program using one of the following methods, depending on whether you are using a hard disk drive or floppy disks:

- If you have installed the program on your hard disk, enter the proper subdirectory, then type PS after the prompt.

- If you are using floppy disks, insert the program disk into drive A, then type PS and press ↵ after the prompt.

When you start The New Print Shop, the first screen that appears is the MAIN MENU (Figure 1.1). Let's examine this screen for a moment. The box on the left contains the menu with the current choices—in

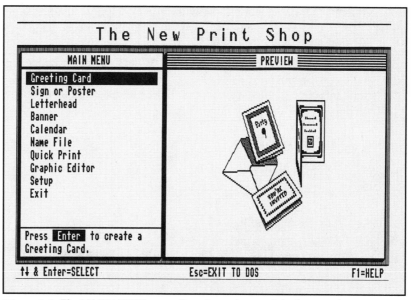

Figure 1.1: The MAIN MENU screen lists the projects and the features that you may select.

this case, the MAIN MENU. The MAIN MENU lists each of the five projects available in The New Print Shop program: Greeting Card, Sign or Poster, Letterhead, Banner, and Calendar. It also lists the new features Name File, Quick Print, and Graphic Editor, as well as Setup (used to set up your printer—see Appendix A for more information) and Exit (the option you choose to quit the program).

You can choose any one of these items on the menu by pressing either ↑ or ↓ to highlight it, then pressing the Enter key (↵).

On the right side of the screen is the PREVIEW box, where you will be able to see your project as you create it. Below the menu is a message area which tells you what to do. Across the bottom of the screen is an information box with additional instructions.

How to Select and Load the Ready-Made Card

Let's begin by starting the program and loading a ready-made card.

1. Start up The New Print Shop.

When you enter the program, the Greeting Card option is highlighted on the menu. The message area below the menu displays this message: Press Enter to Create a Greeting Card. This is the choice you want.

2. Press ↵ to select the Greeting Card project.

The first Greeting Card screen appears. The menu box on the left asks you to choose one of the following items:

> Design Your Own
>
> Use a Ready Made
>
> Load a Saved Card

Design Your Own is highlighted.

3. Press ↓ once to highlight Use a Ready Made, then press ↵ to select it.

The next menu lists only one choice, CARDS. The message box, however, tells you that you can also get ready-made cards from another disk or file. We'll try that later. For now, select CARDS.

4. Press ↵.

The READY MADE screen appears (Figure 1.2) and lists the twelve ready-made cards. A small box in the preview area gives you a brief description of each card.

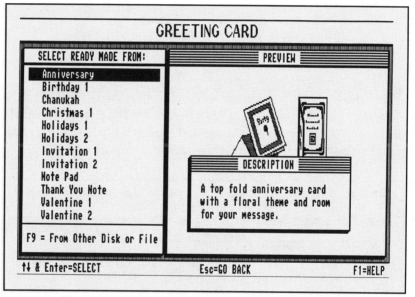

Figure 1.2: The READY MADE screen offers twelve choices and presents a description of each card.

5. Press ↓ one or two times to see the description change.
6. Now press ↑ until Anniversary is highlighted again.
7. Press ↵ to select Anniversary.

A *Look at the GREETING CARD: Front Screen*

The GREETING CARD: Front screen (Figure 1.3) should now be on your monitor. The title bar of this screen reads GREETING CARD: Front, the menu box title is FRONT MENU, and the PREVIEW box displays a picture of the front of the anniversary card.

In the FRONT MENU you have five choices:

Border

Graphic

Message

Inside of Card

Customize

The check marks in the boxes to the left of the Border and Message show that this ready-made card has a border and some text. You could change the border or the message or add a graphic if you desire, but for now let's leave it the way it is and proceed to the inside of the card.

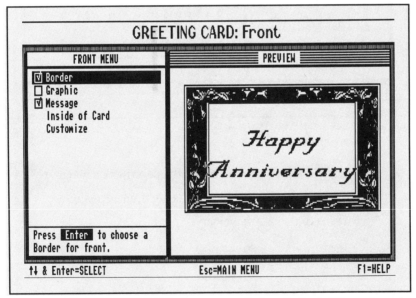

Figure 1.3: The GREETING CARD: Front screen displays the front of the ready-made card and offers five menu choices.

8. Press ↓ three times to highlight Inside of Card, then press ↵ to select it.

How to Modify the Inside of a Ready-Made Card

The GREETING CARD: Inside screen (Figure 1.4) is now on your monitor. It is similar to the GREETING CARD: Front screen. The INSIDE MENU on the left lets you make changes to the inside of your card, which appears in the PREVIEW box.

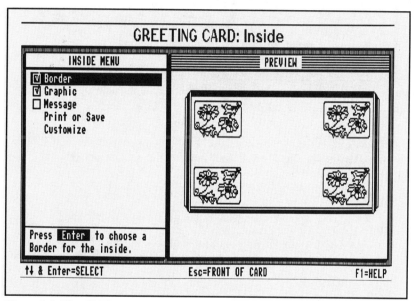

Figure 1.4: The GREETING CARD: Inside screen

Creating a Message

Let's add a message on this page.

9. Press ↓ twice to highlight the word Message, then press ↵.

A list of *fonts* now appears in the left box, with MERCED highlighted (Figure 1.5). This is the font used on the front of the card. A box in the preview area shows you what this font looks like and how big it is. You

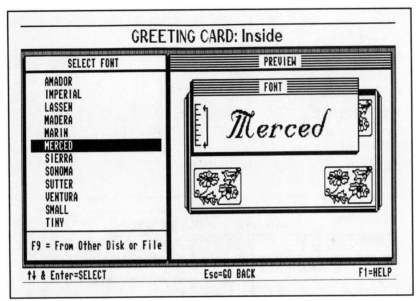

Figure 1.5: *The list of fonts shows the different kinds of type you can use to create your message.*

can choose any of the fonts listed, but for this example let's keep the MERCED font.

10.   Press ↵ to select the MERCED font.

The SELECT STYLE menu (Figure 1.6) should now appear on your screen. You have the opportunity to choose a font style from the following list:

SOLID

OUTLINE

3-D

RAISED

SHADOW

11.   Press ↓ slowly four times to see your choices illustrated in the STYLE box in the preview area.

12.   Press the arrow key one more time to highlight SOLID, then press ↵ to select it.

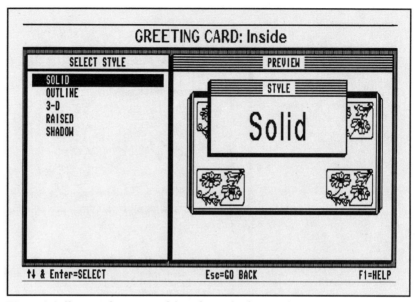

Figure 1.6: You can choose one of these five styles for your font.

A blinking cursor now appears in the PREVIEW box to indicate the place where text will appear when you type it in. Let's add the names Judy and Joe to make the card more personal.

13. Type **Judy & Joe** and leave the cursor on this line of type (don't press ↵).

Now you'll center the message in the middle of the page between the graphics. The EDIT COMMANDS menu lists F8 as the command key for centering text.

14. Press F8 to center the text on the page.

Previewing Your Design

Whenever you want to see what your design will look like on the card, press the F10 key for a preview (Figure 1.7).

15. Press F10 to preview your work.

16. Press any key to return to the EDIT COMMANDS menu.

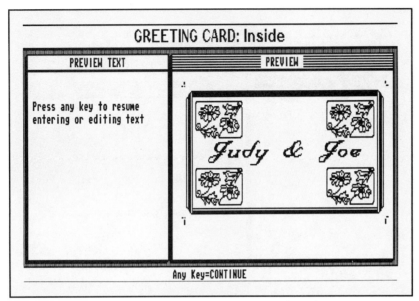

Figure 1.7: When you use the F10 key, the PREVIEW box shows how your current design will look on the finished card.

17. Press Esc to return to the INSIDE MENU.

At this point, you could continue modifying the inside of your card using any one of the commands listed on the current menu. Since we are finished adding a message to this card, let's just return to the IN-SIDE MENU.

Printing Your Finished Ready-Made Card

When the GREETING CARD: Inside screen reappears, Print or Save is highlighted.

18. Press ↵ to select Print or Save.

The PRINT OR SAVE MENU (Figure 1.8) is now on your screen. Let's look at some of the options you have on this menu.

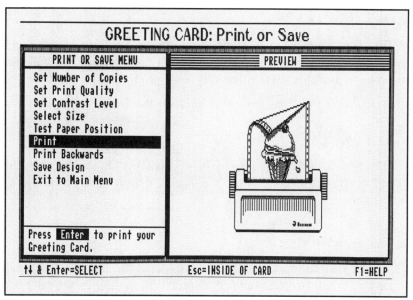

Figure 1.8: The PRINT OR SAVE MENU offers many options for you to consider before printing your card.

Set Number of Copies

The number of copies is already set at 1. Even if you want more than one copy of your card, it is a good idea to print a draft copy to check it. We don't need to change this setting now, so skip this option.

Set Print Quality

The next option on the PRINT MENU is Set Print Quality. Let's select this one.

19. Press ↑ four times to highlight Set Print Quality, then press ↵.

Two choices appear on the menu—Standard Draft Quality and Enhanced Final Quality. Standard Draft Quality prints your card faster, but produces a lighter, grayish product. It is good for checking your work to be sure it is printing correctly. Enhanced Final Quality prints it slower, but produces a darker, sharper image.

20. Press ↓ once, then press ↵ to select Enhanced Final Quality.

Set Contrast Level

The Set Contrast Level option also controls how dark your printed images will be by controlling the density of the printing. You will find this option useful when printing very large products. You don't need to use it now, so let's skip it.

Select Size

The next option on the PRINT MENU is Select Size. You can print greeting cards in several sizes. We'll use this option later in this chapter, but for now we'll skip it.

Test Paper Position

Before printing your card, it is very important to have your paper in your printer at the correct starting position because The New Print Shop prints very close to the edge of the paper. Also, to be able to fold your card correctly, you must print it in the proper place on the paper. The Test Paper Position feature on this print menu allows you to check the position of the paper in your printer.

21. Be sure your printer is turned on and ready to print.

22. Press ↑ once to highlight Test Paper Position, then press ↵.

Your printer will immediately print a row of light dots. If your paper is properly positioned, this line of dots should print on the perforation between two sheets of paper.

If the line is not printing on the perforation, adjust the paper in your printer accordingly. Either roll the paper forward or backward by hand with the platen knob on your printer or advance the paper one or two lines with the line feed control. Then try the test again.

When the dots finally print on the perforation line, you're ready to move on.

23. Press ↓ once to highlight Done, then press ↵.

Print

You are now ready to print your card. When you return to the PRINT MENU, Print is highlighted.

24. Press ↵ to select Print.

Your printer should be printing your card. The printout should look like Figure 1.9.

Saving Your Design

Now that your card is printed, save the file so that you can use it later.

25. Press ↓ twice to highlight Save Design, then press ↵.

You must enter a file name of eight letters or less. Let's name this card JJCARD.

26. Type **JJCARD** and press ↵.

A description box now appears in which you can write a short description of your card. When you retrieve a card you have previously saved, this description will appear in the PREVIEW box. To add a description of your card:

27. Type **ANNIVERSARY CARD FOR JUDY & JOE** and press ↵ to save it.

Exiting The New Print Shop

If you want to start another project, return to the MAIN MENU.

28. Highlight Exit to the Main Menu, then press ↵.

If you feel you need a break before continuing this tutorial, exit the program:

29. Highlight Exit and press ↵.

30. When the dialog box appears asking you to verify that you want to exit the program, highlight Yes, exit to DOS, then press ↵.

Figure 1.9: The printout of your ready-made card.

How to Fold Your Card

Carefully remove your card from the printer. Fold it according to the instructions in Figure 1.10. Both the top-fold and side-fold cards are folded the same way.

Designing Your Own Cards

Designing your own card with The New Print Shop can be almost as easy as using a ready-made card.

First, before you load the program, perhaps even before you turn on your computer, think about the card you want to create. Think about what you want to say and the graphics you might use.

For this example, let's say that you are the Junior Choir director at your church. You want to create a thank-you card for the woman who played the piano every Wednesday afternoon for the last eight months. Before you ask for her help next year, you want her to know how much you appreciate her volunteer efforts.

The piano graphic in The New Print Shop program catches your eye. So does the music staff. Let's use both of them.

If you aren't already in The New Print Shop, load the program onto your computer. Select Greeting Card from the MAIN MENU.

To create your own card, you must select the Design Your Own option from the next menu.

1. Highlight Design Your Own, then press ↵.

The next menu lets you choose the type of fold you want.

2. Press ↵ to select SIDE FOLD.

Creating the Front: Adding a Graphic and Message

Although Border, Graphic, and Message are listed in this order on the FRONT MENU, you can begin with any of these options.

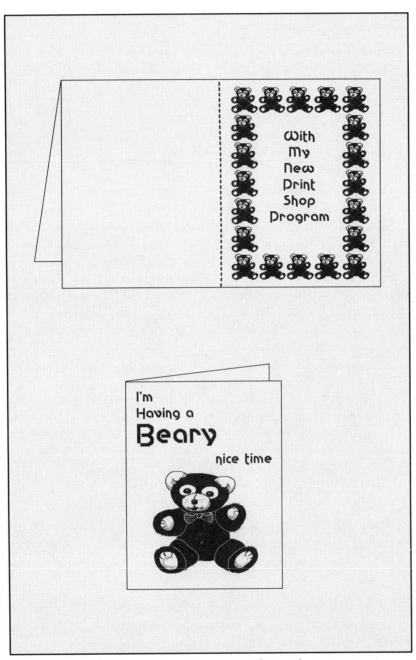

Figure 1.10: *First fold the paper in half to create an 8 1/2 -by-5 1/2 -inch rectangle.
Then fold the paper again.*

Choosing a Graphic

Since you know what graphic you want, let's begin by selecting the graphic for the front of the card.

　　3. Highlight GRAPHIC, then press ↵.

When the GRAPHIC LAYOUT menu (Figure 1.11) appears on your screen, you may want to highlight several of the graphic layout choices listed to explore your layout possibilities.

　　4. Highlight the third choice, Large Centered, then press ↵.

　　5. Press ↵ to select GRAPHICS Hi Res from the next menu.

The SELECT GRAPHIC menu (Figure 1.12) is now on your screen. The menu on the left lists the name of the graphics, and the GRAPHIC box in the preview area shows the corresponding picture.

　　6. Press ↓ slowly to preview the graphics available to you.

You could continue to press ↓ to see your selections, but there are faster ways to move through the list of graphics:

- The End key will move the highlight to the end of the list.
- The Home key will move the highlight to the beginning of the list.
- The Page Down key (Pg Dn) will move down one screen and bring up the new list.
- The Page Up key (Pg Up) will move back to a previous screen.

Now select your graphic.

　　7. Press Pg Dn.

　　8. Highlight PIANO, and then press ↵.

Notice that the graphic appears within a blinking cursor in the preview area. You could change your graphic now by following

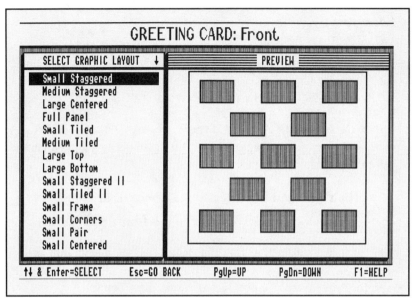

Figure 1.11: The GRAPHIC LAYOUT menu offers many possible layouts for your graphic.

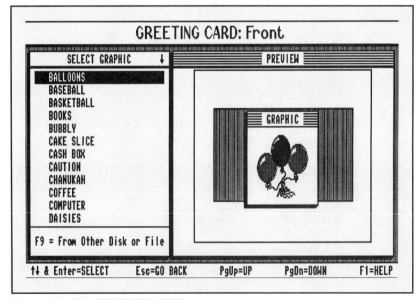

Figure 1.12: The SELECT GRAPHIC menu

the instructions in the menu box. For this card you do not need to modify the graphic.

9. Press ↵ to continue.

Creating the Front Message

When you return to the GREETING CARD: Front screen, a check mark appears in the box beside Graphic to indicate that you have already chosen a graphic, and Message is highlighted. Since we want to add a message to the front of this card, choose this option.

10. Press ↵ to select Message.

The SELECT FONT menu is now on your screen. We will use IMPERIAL font for this design.

11. Press ↓ once to highlight IMPERIAL, then press ↵.
12. Press ↵ to select SOLID on the SELECT STYLE menu.

The most important word in this card is **Thanks**. Let's type it first and make the type large.

13. Press F5 to change the type size to large.

Note that the cursor has expanded to indicate that letters on this line will be bigger.

14. Type **Thanks**.
15. Press ↵ six times to bring the cursor to the line below the piano graphic.

When you pressed ↵ the first time, the size of the cursor changed back to small. Anything you type now will appear in small type unless you press F5 again. Keep the size small for the rest of this page.

16. Type **for your** on this line.
17. Press ↵.

18. Type **HELP**.

19. Press F10 to preview your card.

The preview of the front of your card should look like the one in Figure 1.13.

Experiment with the Layout of Your Card

One of the most important features of The New Print Shop is the ability to change your design and experiment to see what you like best. Let's change a few things on this design to see how easy it is.

There is too much white space between the type and the graphic. You have several ways to change this. One way is to simply retype the word **Thanks** on the next line.

20. Press any key to end the preview.

21. Press ↑ seven times to put the cursor back on the line with the word **Thanks**.

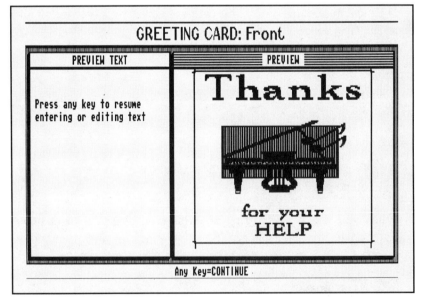

Figure 1.13: When you have finished creating the message, you can preview your design to see if you want to make changes.

22. Backspace six times to erase **Thanks**.

23. Press F5 to change the typesize back to small.

24. Press ↵ to drop the cursor down a line.

25. Press F5 again for large typesize.

26. Type **Thanks**.

27. Press F10 to preview your card again.

Moving the Graphic

That's better, but the piano graphic is still too far from the bottom type. Let's try moving the graphic to get rid of this white space.

28. Press any key to continue.

29. Press Esc to leave the EDIT COMMANDS menu.

30. Press ↓ to highlight Customize, then press ↵.

A dialog box now asks if you want to save a copy of your creation before customizing. This is a good idea. If you make changes you don't like you can then go back to the original without starting over from the beginning.

31. Press ↵ to save a copy of your card.

When you enter Customize, a blinking box, or cursor, appears around the piano graphic. This cursor indicates which part of your design you can change at this time. You can move the blinking box with the arrow keys to select another part of your design. However, the piano graphic is what you want to change now, so leave the cursor where it is.

The current menu lists M as the Move command key.

32. Press M on your keyboard to move the piano graphic.

Now new instructions appear in the menu box that tell you how to move the graphic with the arrow keys.

33. Press ↓ once.

Notice that the blinking cursor moves, not the graphic.

   34. Press ↵ to move the graphic to the new cursor location.

That's better. The piano graphic has moved closer to the text.

The Customize option offers many other creative opportunities besides moving your graphic, and these are fully discussed in Chapter 9.
For now, let's move on to the inside of your card.

   35. Press Esc to return to the FRONT MENU.

   36. Press ↑ once to highlight Inside of Card, then press ↵.

Creating the Inside: Using a Graphics Frame and Thin Border

You'll start designing the inside of the card by selecting a graphic
layout.

Framing Your Card Using Small Graphics

One interesting choice in the SELECT GRAPHIC LAYOUT menu
in The New Print Shop is the Small Frame option, which gives you
the ability to create a frame or border with any graphic. Let's select this
option.

   37. Press ↓ to highlight Graphic, then press ↵.

   38. Press ↓ ten times to highlight Small Frame, then press ↵.

   39. Press ↵ to select GRAPHICS Hi Res from the next menu.

Now let's try a faster way to select the graphic than scrolling down
the screen. Look on the card of designs that came with The New Print
Shop program. Note that each graphic has a number. Find the picture of
the music staff. Its number is 22.

   40. Press F2.

A small box appears in the center of your screen. Its title reads SELECT BY NUMBER (Figure 1.14). A blinking cursor indicates where you will type in the number of the graphic.

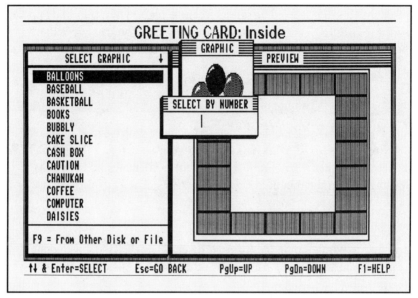

Figure 1.14: When you press F2, the SELECT BY NUMBER box appears to let you choose a graphic by number.

41. Type 22.

42. Press ↵ to enter your selection.

The music graphic now appears in the GRAPHIC box, and the word MUSIC is highlighted in the menu box.

43. Press ↵ two times, once to select the graphics and once to return to the INSIDE MENU.

Choosing a Thin Border

Sometimes the small graphics frame pattern creates a nice border by itself. But in the case of our card, the frame will look more unified with a thin border around it.

44. Highlight BORDER, then press ↵.

45. Press ↵ to select THIN BORDER from the next menu.

THIN LINE, the first choice of ten thin border styles listed in the menu box, is highlighted on your screen. A picture of a thin line appears in the BORDER box within the preview area. You can view the other border styles in this box by using ↓ to scroll down the menu.

46. Highlight THIN LINE if it isn't still highlighted, then press ↵.

Creating the Inside Message

Now the INSIDE MENU is back on your screen and the PREVIEW box shows the graphic frame with a thin border around it. Message is highlighted on the menu.

47. Press ↵ to select Message.

The font you used on the front of the card, IMPERIAL, is the one that is highlighted as your first choice for the inside. Let's choose it again for the inside.

48. Press ↵ to select IMPERIAL from the list of fonts.

49. Press ↵ to select SOLID from the SELECT STYLE menu.

50. Type the following words as shown. Remember to press ↵ at the end of each line, but do not press it after **Choir** on the last line.

    with

    the

    Junior

    Choir

51. Press F8 to center the type top to bottom on the page.

52. Press F10 to preview your card.

The preview of your card should look like Figure 1.15.

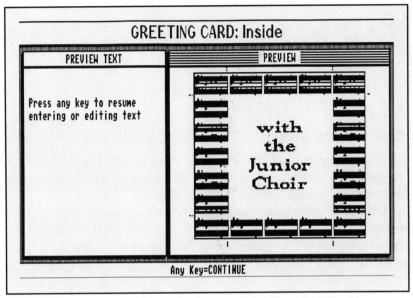

Figure 1.15: The preview of the inside of your card should now look like this.

53. Press any key to end the preview.

54. Press Esc to return to the INSIDE MENU.

Giving Yourself Credit

When you have finished designing the card, you are almost ready to print and save it. Before you do, let's add a one-line credit to the back of the card. You can do this with the Give Yourself Credit option on the PRINT OR SAVE MENU. This option is not available on top-fold cards. On commercial cards the one-line credit is usually reserved for the card company's name.

55. Print or Save is already highlighted on the INSIDE MENU. Press ↵ to select it.

56. Press ↑ six times to move the highlight to the top of the menu to Give Yourself Credit, then press ↵.

You can add any credit you want. For now let's type the following one:

57. Type **The Music Department**.

58. Press ↵ to enter it.

Printing Your Designed Card

Before you print your card, test the print position as you did when you printed a ready-made card. Be sure the test line of dots prints on the perforation line between two sheets of paper.

Remember, it is a good idea to print out a draft-quality copy to check to see that everything is the way you want it. The draft quality prints a lighter copy but prints it faster. Since the draft quality is the default setting, you do not need to do anything to choose it. Print your card using the same procedure you followed for printing the ready-made card.

The side-fold card prints out in a different position on the page than the top-fold card. The first part to emerge from your printer is upside down. Your printout should look like Figure 1.16.

When your draft is finished, carefully check the printout for errors. If there is anything you want to change, you may press the Esc key and return to your design. If it is correct, set the print quality to Enhanced Final Quality, and print out a final copy.

Saving Your Card to Another Disk

You may want to save all of your creations on one disk. Since it is so easy to load previously created cards back onto your screen, you can reuse them again and again.

To save your design, return to the PRINT OR SAVE MENU.

59. Press ↓ twice to highlight Save Design, then press ↵.

If you have more than one drive and you want to save your cards on a special disk:

60. Press F9 to change drives.

61. Highlight the drive containing the disk you want to save to, then press ⏎.

62. Type a file name of eight letters or less, then press ⏎.

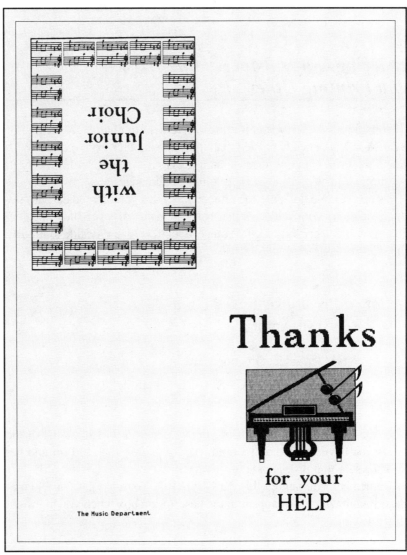

Figure 1.16:A side-fold card will be printed with the first part, the inside, up-side down.

63. Next, type in a longer description when prompted so that you will be able to identify your card when you need it. Press ↵.

Now that you have finished this project, exit to the MAIN MENU to either go on to the next section or exit The New Print Shop.

Retrieving Cards from Another Disk and Printing Other Sizes

Sometimes you may find it more convenient to change the design of a card you have already created than to design another from scratch. With The New Print Shop, you can load a previously saved card, modify it, and reuse it. You can also reprint it in a smaller size.

As an example, let's use the anniversary card you created earlier. Say that a neighbor calls and says that he's having a party for Judy and Joe, and everyone is bringing a gift. You need a gift card and decide to modify the card you already sent.

Loading a Previously Saved Card

Start at the MAIN MENU.

1. Press ↵ to select Greeting Card.

2. On the GREETING CARD screen, highlight Load a Saved Card, then press ↵.

In the menu box on the left of your screen you will see a list of the cards you have created and stored. (If you stored the card on another disk, be sure that disk is in your drive.)

Remember you named this card JJCARD. You also gave it a longer description, which will appear in the description box when you highlight this selection.

3. Highlight JJCARD and press ↵.

*C*hanging the Saved Card

You can now change any part of the anniversary card. Let's change the inside by deleting the graphics to make room for a message.

4. On the FRONT MENU, highlight Inside of Card, then press ↵.

5. Highlight Graphic, then press ↵.

A dialog box now appears on your screen (Figure 1.17) to remind you that you have already selected graphics and gives you the following choices:

Modify your Layout and Graphics

Choose a new Layout and Graphics

Delete all Graphics

Cancel

6. Press ↓ twice to select Delete all Graphics, then press ↵.

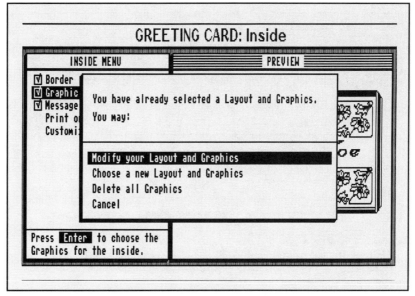

Figure 1.17: When you have already chosen graphics and want to change something, this dialog box will appear on the screen when you select Graphic again.

Now add another name to the inside. Return to the INSIDE MENU.

7. Highlight Message on the INSIDE MENU, and press ↵.

Another dialog box appears (Figure 1.18) with these choices:

> Edit your Text
>
> Enter all new Text
>
> Delete the Text
>
> Cancel

Edit your Text is already highlighted.

8. Press ↵ to select Edit your Text.

9. Press F8 to turn off the centering command; this moves the current text to the top line to make room for more text.

10. Press ↵, then type **From**.

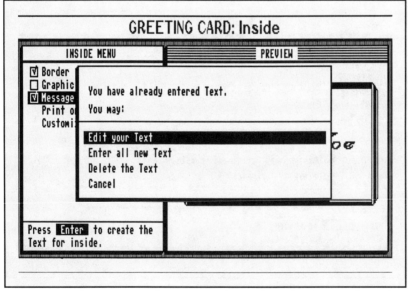

Figure 1.18: When you try to select Message after you have already created text, this dialog box appears on your screen.

11. Press ⏎ to proceed to the next line.

12. Type in your own name. Do not press ⏎ at the end of this line.

13. Press F8 to center the type again.

14. Press Esc again to return to the GREETING CARD: Inside screen.

*P*rinting Your Card in a Smaller Size

In The New Print Shop, your cards will automatically be printed out in full size (4¼-by-5½ inches) unless you select a different size from the SELECT SIZE menu. To print your card in a size smaller than full size, first proceed to the PRINT OR SAVE MENU.

15. Since Print or Save is already highlighted on your menu, press ⏎ to select it.

16. Highlight Set Print Quality, then press ⏎.

17. Press ↓ to highlight Enhanced Final Quality, and then press ⏎.

18. Once you return to the PRINT OR SAVE MENU, press ↑ twice to highlight Select Size, then press ⏎.

A list of six sizes now appears in the menu box:

> Full Size (100%)
>
> Large (80%)
>
> Medium (75%)
>
> Small (67%)
>
> Tiny (50%)
>
> Very Tiny (33%)

Appendix B shows a comparison of these sizes. For this example we will choose Small.

19. Highlight SMALL, then press ⏎.

Turn on your printer and test the paper position if you need to. If you have not printed anything since printing the cards in the first two examples, your paper is probably still in the correct position. Now print your card.

How to Fold Smaller Cards

The smaller sizes are folded the same way as the full sizes. The first fold is across the 8½-inch side of the paper, and the second fold is across the 11-inch side. Use the edge of the paper as a cutting guide when cropping off the excess paper. See Figure 1.19 for a diagram.

Enhancing Your Cards with Additional Options

The Greeting Card project has many more options than you explored in these three examples. Without completing a full product, let's discuss some additional things you can do to further enhance the appearance of your cards.

Using Wide Borders

When you create your own design, you can use either thin or wide borders. The New Print Shop comes with five wide borders. You can choose them by selecting Borders from either the GREETING CARD: Front or GREETING CARD: Inside screens.

With a wide border you may not need another graphic. Just type your message as you did on the anniversary card we used in the previous examples.

You may use this same wide border on the front and inside. Or, you may want to use it only on the front and select a thin border or no border for the inside. Although you could choose one wide border for the front and another for the inside, this would not produce an attractive card.

Using a wide border, such as Lilies or Holly, and no additional graphic or message on the front, you could create a frame for a photograph. After you print your card, cut out the space within the frame. Insert the

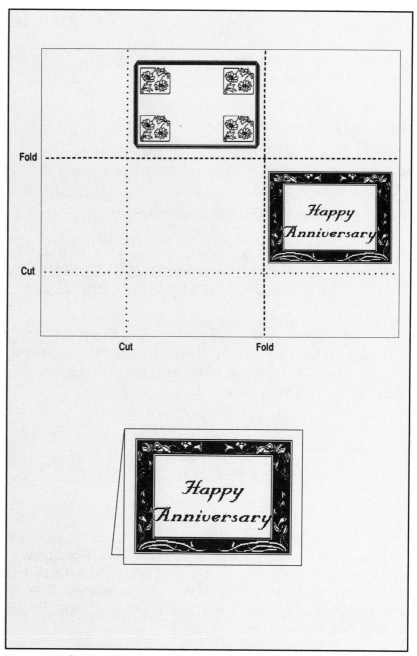

Figure 1.19: Smaller sizes of greeting cards are folded the same way as the full size. Use the edge of the paper as a cutting guide when trimming your card.

photo behind it. You can anchor the photo in place with a little rubber cement or glue stick.

Photo cards of a team or contest winner are a nice way to show appreciation to a sponsor.

Using Full Panels

There are ten vertical full panel designs available to use with side-fold cards and five horizontal ones to use with top-fold cards.

Selecting and Previewing a Full Panel Graphic

Next you'll explore the possibilities of full panels. Once in the Greeting Card project, select Design Your Own, then choose SIDE FOLD. Select Graphic from the GREETING CARD: Front screen. Full Panel is the fourth choice listed on the SELECT GRAPHIC LAYOUT menu.

1. Highlight Full Panel, then press ↵.

You will now see a list of the full panels available. In the PREVIEW box there is also a description of the full panel that is highlighted. Let's take a look at the SCHOOL panel.

2. Highlight SCHOOL.

3. Press F10 to preview this panel.

4. Press any key to exit the preview, then press ↵ to select this design.

Positioning Text on a Full Panel

Positioning text on a full panel can be a little tricky. When the centered type runs into part of the graphic, you may have to delete the line and add a few spaces before retyping the words as illustrated in the invitation for an open house in Figure 1.20. Let's experiment with this text on the SCHOOL panel.

5. On the GREETING CARD: Front screen, highlight Message in the menu box, then press ↵.
6. On the SELECT FONT menu, highlight SONOMA, then press ↵.

Figure 1.20: You can fine-tune the spacing on full panels by using the spacebar to put in extra spaces.

7. On the SELECT STYLE menu, press ↵ to select SOLID.

A cursor is blinking on the first line. Let's start our message on the next line.

8. Press ↵ to place the cursor on the second line.

9. On the next four lines, type the following message, remembering to press ↵ at the end of each word:

   Welcome

   our new

   foreign

   exchange

10. Press the F10 key to preview your work.

Notice that the word exchange runs into the apple. Let's correct this by adding extra spaces before the word.

11. Press any key to return to the EDIT COMMANDS menu.

12. Press ↑ to move the cursor to **exchange**.

13. Press the Backspace key eight times to delete the word.

14. Press the spacebar twice and then type **exchange**.

15. Press F10 to preview your design.

16. Press any key to continue.

When you try to enter text on the next line, a dialog box will appear telling you that you have run out of space for your message and are about to exit. On the outer edges of the card you can see small margin tabs. These indicate where the card's margins are. Note that the cursor rests below the tabs for the bottom margin. To make more room for your text, you must lower the bottom margin.

17. Highlight Go Back to Editing, then press ↵.

18. Press F7 to change margins.

19. Highlight Move Bottom Margin, and press ↵.

A blinking cursor cuts across the lower part of the card.

   20. Press ↓ twice to move the bottom margin.

Notice that only the cursor moves. Accept the cursor position as the new bottom margin.

   21. Press ↵.

The margin tabs now appear closer to the bottom of your card.
   You will also need to move the right margin to fit the next word in.

   22. On this same menu, highlight RIGHT MARGIN, then press ↵.

A vertical cursor now appears through the right side of the card.

   23. Press → once to move the right margin.
   24. Press ↵.

Now that you have finished changing the margins,

   25. Press ↓ three times to highlight Done, then press ↵.

When you return to the message workspace:

   26. Press ↵ to move the cursor to the next line, press the spacebar five times, and then type **student**.
   27. Press F10 to preview your design.
   28. Press any key to continue.
   29. Press Esc to exit the EDIT COMMANDS menu.

How to Use More Than One Graphic and Change a Layout

Perhaps the layouts available for graphics don't fit the idea you have, or you want to use more than one graphic on either the front or inside.

Figure 1.21 shows a card with a graphic of a computer and another of a printer. To accomplish this, follow the steps below.

1. From the Greeting Card screen, select Design Your Own.

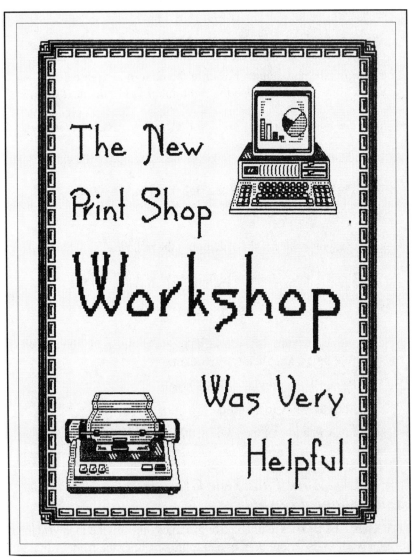

Figure 1.21: You can have more than one graphic on a page and make changes in the standard layouts.

2. Select the side-fold card from the next menu.

3. Choose Graphic from the FRONT MENU.

4. Highlight the Medium Staggered layout, then press ↵.

5. Highlight GRAPHICS Hi Res, then press ↵.

6. Press ↓ ten times to highlight COMPUTER, then press ↵.

You now have five computer graphics on your screen in the Medium Staggered layout. A blinking cursor surrounds the first one. Let's erase this graphic.

7. Press the spacebar once to turn off the graphic within the cursor.

8. Press ↓ once to move the cursor to the middle computer.

9. Press the spacebar once to erase it, too.

10. Press ↓ once to move the cursor to the computer in the lower-left corner.

Let's change this one to a printer.

11. Press C.

When you have the graphic menu on your screen, the GRAPHIC box appears where the cursor was. Scrolling down the menu changes the graphic in the box.

12. Press Pg Dn to get to PRINTER.

13. Highlight PRINTER, then press ↵.

The computer graphic in the lower-left corner has been replaced by a picture of a printer. Let's erase the lower-right computer.

14. Press → once to highlight the lower-right computer.

15. Press the spacebar to erase it.

16. Press ↵ to return to the FRONT MENU.

Place a thin border around this page to hold this design together.

17. Highlight Border, then press ↵.

18. Highlight THIN, then press ↵.

19. Highlight BLOCKS, then press ↵.

As you can see in the PREVIEW box, the computer graphic is now too close to the border. To move it:

20. Highlight Customize on the GREETING CARD: Front screen, and then press ↵.

21. Select Enter Customize without saving when the dialog box appears.

22. Press ↓ once to highlight the computer.

23. Press M on your keyboard to move the graphic.

24. Press ↓ once and ← once, then press ↵ to accept the change.

25. Press Esc to return to the FRONT MENU.

Now let's create a message around the graphic layout.

26. Highlight Message, then press ↵.

27. Highlight LASSEN from the SELECT FONT menu, then press ↵.

28. Select SOLID from the next menu.

29. Press F6 to position text on the left side of the card.

30. Press ↵ to drop down one line.

The type will be too close to the border on the left if you just start typing. Use a blank space to position the type just as you did in the full panel example.

31. Press the spacebar once and type **The New**.

32. Press ↵ to begin a new line.

33. Press the spacebar once and type **Print Shop**.

34. Press ↵ to begin a new line.

Let's use a large type across the middle of the card.

35. Press F5 to use a larger type.

36. Press F6 twice to center this line of type.

37. Type **Workshop**.

Now let's create two lines for the lower-right corner of the page. Just as the top lines were too close to the border without an extra space, these lines will be, too, unless you add the extra space at the end. Let's try it.

38. Press ↵ to begin a new line.

39. Press F6 twice to position text on the right side of the card.

40. Type **Was Very** and press the spacebar once.

41. Press ↵ to begin a new line.

42. Type **Helpful** and press the spacebar once.

43. Press F10 to preview your design.

Your design should now look like Figure 1.21.

Experimenting with Fonts

The New Print Shop allows you to vary the type on a page in the following ways:

- You can change the font on every line.
- You can use up to six fonts on one page.
- You can change the size and style on any line.
- You can place the type anywhere on the page.

You will now create a card front that demonstrates some of the things you can do and lets you see some of the different fonts and styles.

1. From the Greeting Card screen, select Design Your Own, then choose side-fold again.

2. Select Message from the FRONT MENU.

3. From the SELECT FONT menu choose AMADOR.

4. From the SELECT STYLE menu choose SOLID.

5. Press F6 to align the type on the left side.

6. Type **Because** and press ↵.

7. Press F6 twice to center the cursor again.

8. Press F5 for large type.

9. Type **You Can** and press ↵.

10. On the following five lines, type the following message, remembering to press ↵ at the end of each line:

    change font

    size and style

    on every line

    doesn't mean

    You Should

Now go back and change the fonts with the F3 key and the styles with the F4 key. You can use any combination you wish. To get the illustration in Figure 1.22, use the following fonts and styles:

You Can (SUTTER, OUTLINE)

change font (MARIN, SOLID)

size and style (MERCED, RAISED)

on every line (SONOMA, SOLID)

doesn't mean (VENTURA, SOLID)

You Should (AMADOR, 3-D)

Note that because The New Print Shop only allows you to use six font styles on a page, when you go to select a font for the final line, a dialog box appears reminding you to choose one of the fonts you've already picked.

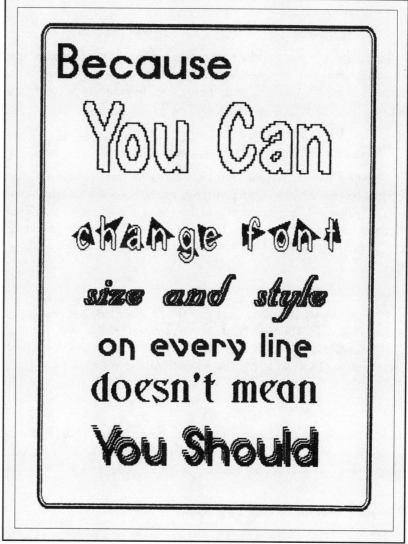

Figure 1.22: *The New Print Shop lets you change the font, style, and size of type on every line.*

Where to Find More Ideas for Enhancing Your Cards

There are many more ideas that you can use when creating cards in some of the other chapters in this book.

Print Personalized Cards Easily with Name File

Perhaps you'd like to print out several copies of the same card, each personalized with a person's name on the front or inside. Learn how to create a name file that will print these cards automatically. See Chapter 6.

Getting the Most Out of the Customize Option

Perhaps you would like to shrink some type to make it fit in a design. Or maybe you'd like to enlarge it. You might need to flip graphics so that they face another direction. Maybe you'd like to use two different size graphics on a single page. There are instructions for these features of Customize and many more ideas in Chapter 9.

Adding Extra Graphics and Fonts

Perhaps you would like to add more pictures, borders, and panels than are available with The New Print Shop program. Perhaps you would like a wider choice of fonts. There are several ways you can add to your collection of graphics and fonts. These are discussed in Chapter 10.

Printing Tips

Maybe you would like to print your card on colored paper or with colored ribbons. The New Print Shop has the ability to print in color. Learn more about additional printing options in Chapter 14.

Creating Special Effects with a Photocopier

If you need to produce a large number of cards, or add a logo, you can create special effects with the aid of a good photocopy machine. See Chapter 14.

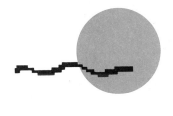

2 Making Signs and Posters

The Sign or Poster project of the original Print Shop was one of the most popular features of the program. With the added features in The New Print Shop, this project could become the most used option of the new version.

Let's take a look at the capabilities of this new version of the project and experiment with a few examples to explore its potential.

The Sign or Poster project gives you the ability to create vertical or horizontal signs and posters. You can produce flyers as small as a single 8½-by-11-inch page or huge wall-size signs as large as 85-by-110 inches.

Choose a ready-made sign from the six that come with the program and customize it, or design one of your own. Any of the graphics, fonts, wide borders, and full panels that come with The New Print Shop can be used to create these signs.

As in the Greeting Card project, you can use up to six fonts and several graphics on one page. These graphics can be many sizes.

While you are designing your sign or poster, you can see your creation in the PREVIEW box on the right side of your screen.

And, you can use the Sign or Poster project to create many other products besides signs and posters.

To understand the potential of this project, let's create a few products. In the following sections, you will learn to create certificates for many occasions and signs for a refreshment stand. You'll discover how to create and assemble huge signs and how to print backwards for heat-transfer designs.

In the additional options section, you learn how to design signs that can lay flat on a table or other horizontal surface and create other products by using only graphics, borders, or words.

Getting Ideas from the Ready-Made Signs

The New Print Shop comes with six ready-made signs that you can use as is or modify for your own purposes. These signs are provided to give you an idea of what you can do with this project. Let's study them for a moment to see what ideas they present:

- You can use the Certificate as a document of merit. It includes enough space for you to add a name. The blue ribbon is a graphic inserted in the Customize feature.

- The Garage Sale sign shows you one way to use multiple graphics to make a sale sign more interesting.

- The Party sign suggests how you can use a full panel and merely fill in your own information to create an announcement.

- The Meeting sign demonstrates the use of a wide border to help call attention to your announcement.

- The Sale sign shows one way you can quickly advertise a sale.

- The Department Meeting Sign shows how you can erase some parts of a graphics layout, in this case the Small Tiled layout, for an interesting effect.

Instead of simply printing out one of these signs, let's see how you can use some of the ideas listed above in your own creations.

Designing Your Own Signs

Let's begin exploring the Signs or Posters project with examples that use the basic 8½-by-11-inch sheet of paper. We'll try creating a certificate similar to one of the ready-made signs.

Creating a Certificate

To create the certificate, you will use the full panel graphic CERTIF. This gives you a fancy ornate border and the word **Certificate** across the top.

Starting with this full panel, you could create many products for many occasions. You could design:

- Certificates of recognition, which can be given to employees or members for outstanding service or years of work. It could also be used to acknowledge contest winners.
- Certificates of appreciation, which can be awarded to a sponsor of your organization or sponsor of a special event.
- Certificates of participation, which can be presented to exhibitors or others who took part in a promotion your organization sponsored.
- Certificates of achievement, which can be used at the end of any workshop or training session, as well as for a personal graduation from a preschool or church school class.

Let's create a certificate of achievement (Figure 2.1) for an employee who completed a workshop on computer training.

1. If you haven't already done so, bring up The New Print Shop on your computer.
2. On the MAIN MENU, highlight Sign or Poster as shown in Figure 2.2, then press ↵ to select it.

Design Your Own is already highlighted on the next menu.

3. Press ↵ to select Design Your Own.

To create a certificate that will print out vertically on a page, you need to choose the Tall sign option. This option is already highlighted on the next menu.

4. Press ↵ to select Tall.

The SIGN MENU (Figure 2.3) should now be on your screen. It is quite similar to the FRONT MENU and INSIDE MENU in the Greeting Card project. The menu box on the left lists your choices, and the

Figure 2.1: You can create a certificate of achievement for any workshop or training session.

PREVIEW box on the right allows you to view your design as you create it.

Although Border is the first choice listed, you do not need a border for this product since a border is included in the full panel. Go directly to Graphic.

    5. Highlight Graphic, then press ↵.

The SELECT GRAPHIC LAYOUT menu (Figure 2.4) offers many possible selections for arranging graphics on your signs and posters. You can choose small, medium, or large graphics and determine how they will be placed on a page.

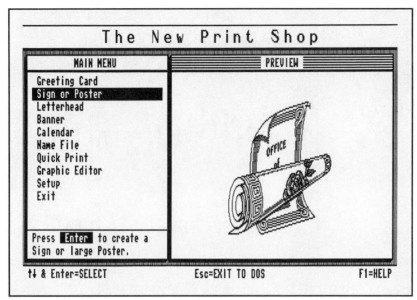

Figure 2.2: You begin using the Sign or Poster project by selecting it from the MAIN MENU.

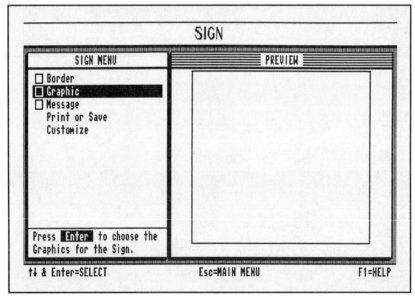

Figure 2.3: The SIGN MENU on the left lists your choices. The PREVIEW box on the right allows you to view your work as you create it.

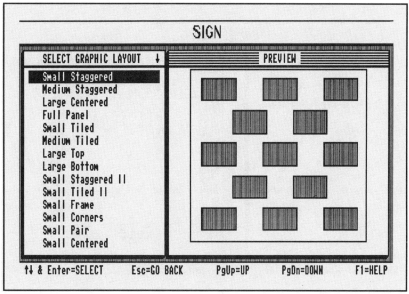

Figure 2.4: The SELECT GRAPHIC LAYOUT menu allows you to choose the size and placement of the graphics.

6. Highlight Full Panel, then press ↵.

CERTIF is the choice that is highlighted. Before you select it, you can preview it to be sure it is the one you want.

7. Press the F10 key to preview the CERTIF full panel. Your screen should look like Figure 2.5.

8. Press any key to exit the preview.

9. Press ↵ to select CERTIF.

When you return to the SIGN MENU, a check mark appears beside Graphic to indicate that you have finished selecting a graphic. Message is now highlighted.

10. Press ↵ to select Message.

When the SELECT FONT menu (Figure 2.6) appears on your screen, you will have the opportunity to select the kind of type you want to use on your certificate. Let's begin with SIERRA.

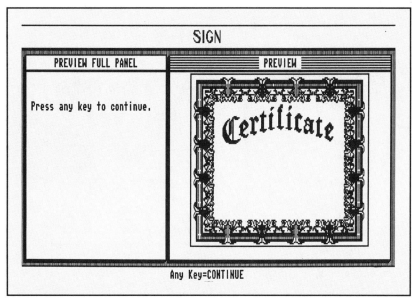

Figure 2.5: You can preview any full panel before you choose it.

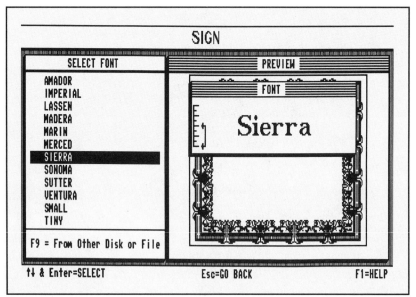

Figure 2.6: The SELECT FONT menu lists the typefaces you can use in your sign or poster.

11.   Highlight SIERRA, then press ↵.

You may now choose the style of type you want from the SELECT STYLE menu (Figure 2.7). SOLID is highlighted on the next menu.

12.   Press ↵ to select SOLID.

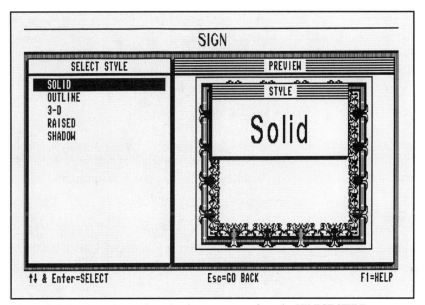

Figure 2.7: You can choose the style of type you want from the SELECT STYLE menu.

When you begin to create your message, the cursor is centered on the line below the word **Certificate**.

13.   Type **of**.

14.   Press ↵ to begin a new line.

15.   Type **Achievement**.

16.   Press ↵ to begin a new line.

For the next line, change the type to a small font.

17.   Press F3 to return to the SELECT FONT menu.

18. Highlight the last selection, TINY, then press ↵.

19. Type **Awarded to** and press ↵.

Because this font is so small, it won't show up on the PREVIEW box. Instead, a series of lines appears on the card to show message placement, and a composition at the bottom of the screen displays the actual message.

The recipient's name should be in a fancy type. If you want, a person's name can be hand-lettered in fancy calligraphy. Here you'll use a nice script.

20. Press the F3 key to return to the SELECT FONT menu.

21. Highlight MERCED, then press ↵.

Many times when you create a certificate you will have a name that is too long to fit in the space. Sometimes you will have to use two lines. But, if the name is only a few letters too long, you can usually find a way to fit it in. We'll use a long name in this example to show one way you can do it.

First, you will need to change the margins (Figure 2.8). Later, when your message is complete, you can shrink or reduce this line in Customize.

22. Press F7 to change margins.

23. Press ↓ twice to highlight Move Left Margin, then press ↵.

A blinking cursor now appears on the left side of the certificate.

24. Press ← twice, then press ↵ to accept the cursor position as the new margin.

25. Press ↓ once more to select Move Right Margin, then press ↵.

A blinking cursor now appears on the right side of the certificate.

26. Press → twice, then press ↵ to accept the cursor position as the new margin.

27. Press ↓ three times to highlight Done, then press ↵ to select it.

28. Type **Al Schlenkowitz** and press ↵.

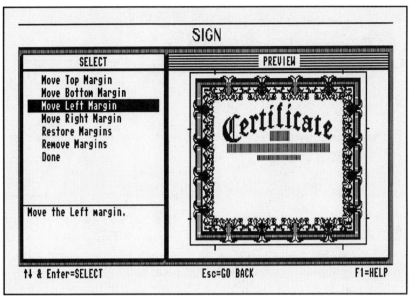

Figure 2.8: You can change the margins on full panels to help you position type.

In the next line, use the TINY font again.

29. Press F3.

30. Highlight TINY, then press ↵.

31. Type **For Completing Workshop in**.

32. Press ↵ to begin a new line.

Now change back to the SIERRA font for the name of the workshop.

33. Press F3.

34. Highlight SIERRA, then press ↵.

35. Type the next two lines, pressing ↵ after the first line but not after the second:

Computer

Training

Before you leave this message workplace, be sure your design is the way you want it.

36. Preview your design by pressing F10.

37. Press any key to end the preview.

38. Press Esc to return to the SIGN MENU.

Customizing

Now you'll use the Customize feature to adjust the name so it does not overlap the borders.

39. Highlight CUSTOMIZE, then press ↵.

A dialog box appears on your screen (Figure 2.9) asking if you want to save your design before entering Customize. This is always a good idea if you have spent a lot of time creating it. If you should be un-happy with some changes, you can always return to this version of your product by selecting Restore from the Customize menu. This is a

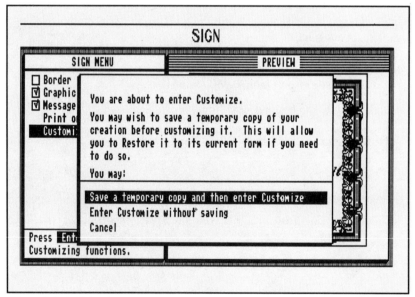

Figure 2.9: A dialog box appears on your screen before you enter Customize to allow you to make a temporary copy of the current version of your creation.

temporary save and will be erased when you leave Customize. It is not a substitute for saving your design later.

40. Press ↵ to save a temporary copy of your design.

When you enter Customize, a blinking box, or cursor, surrounds the border. This blinking cursor identifies the part of the design you wish to change. You need to move it to a line of text (Figure 2.10).

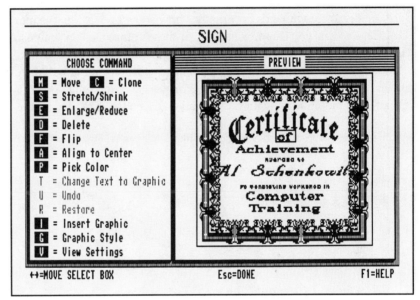

Figure 2.10: In Customize you can make many changes to your design.

41. Press ↓ to select the first line of text.

You can easily manipulate the text with some of the commands used for graphics (these are the options currently in gray on your menu). In order to be able to use these commands with text, you must first change the text to graphics. Use the menu choice T to do this.

42. Press T to change the text to a graphic.

A dialog box now displays this message:

> You are about to convert ALL of your Text to Graphics.
> This will allow you to use all of the customizing functions

reserved for Graphics but you will no longer be able to edit the Text.

Convert the Text to Graphic is highlighted.

43. Press ⏎ to convert the text to graphic.

44. Press ↓ three times to highlight the name line.

Note that the commands for graphics now show up black in the menu box. This means you can now use any of these commands on your card. To make the name line fit the card, you could either reduce or shrink it. Reducing it makes it smaller proportionally, while shrinking will distort the horizontal or vertical size. If the distortion is not too great, it is often easier to use the Shrink feature for small adjustments. Let's try it here.

45. Press S to choose Stretch/Shrink.

A blinking cursor appears around the name.

46. Press ← three times.

Only the cursor shrinks until you press ⏎ to accept the change.

47. Press ⏎.

48. Press A to center the line.

49. From the next menu, choose H for horizontal alignment.

50. Press Esc to return to the SIGN MENU.

Printing the Certificate

You are now ready to print your certificate and can proceed to the PRINT OR SAVE MENU.

51. Highlight Print or Save on the SIGN MENU, then press ⏎.

The PRINT OR SAVE MENU for the Sign or Poster project (Figure 2.11) is quite similar to the one for the Greeting Card project. For one-page projects, such as this example, follow the same procedure for printing as discussed in Chapter 1 and outlined here:

First, set the print quality. Test your paper position before you print. While the printing position is not as critical as in the Greeting Card project, it is important to have the poster print out in the right place on the paper. Once the dots are on the perforation line, print your certificate. The printout should look like the one in Figure 2.1.

When your certificate is printed, you can save the file so that you can use it later for another workshop. Just select Save Design from the PRINT OR SAVE MENU, type in a file name of eight letters or less and a description when prompted, then press ↵.

If you have many certificates to print, you may want to use the Name File feature in The New Print Shop to create a list of names to merge automatically with your design and print them all at one time. For more information on how to do this, see Chapter 6.

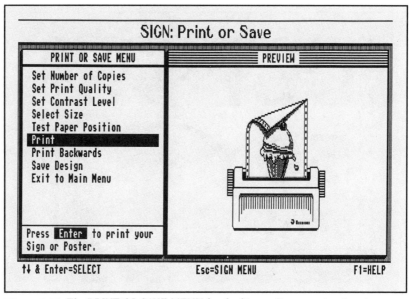

Figure 2.11: The PRINT OR SAVE MENU for the Sign or Poster project is quite
similar to the one for the Greeting Card project.

Creating Signs for a Refreshment Stand

One popular use for signs is to state the prices of items for sale. Many organizations often provide refreshment stands at the county fair. Or parents may volunteer to raise money with a stand at the local 4-H horse show or the high school basketball game. You could print out individual signs in The New Print Shop or stack several in a row.

Printing a Single Sign

Let's begin with a single sign as shown in Figure 2.12 to explore more of the capabilities of The New Print Shop.

1. From the MAIN MENU highlight Sign or Poster, then press ↵.

2. Highlight Design Your Own in the next menu, then press ↵.

3. Highlight Wide from the TYPE OF SIGN menu, then press ↵.

Figure 2.12: You can create single signs for the items you have for sale at a refreshment stand.

This time begin with the border. It is already highlighted when the menu first comes on your screen.

    4. Press ↵ to select Border.

    5. Highlight THIN, then press ↵.

    6. Highlight FRILLY, then press ↵.

When you return to the SIGN MENU, a border is displayed in the PREVIEW box and the word Graphic is now highlighted. It's time to select the graphic.

    7. Press ↵ to proceed to the SELECT GRAPHIC LAYOUT menu.

    8. Highlight Medium Bottom, then press ↵.

GRAPHICS Hi Res is highlighted on the next menu. This is the file that contains the graphics you want.

    9. Press ↵ to select GRAPHICS Hi Res.

Select the coffee cup graphic using the graphic selection box and the number of the graphic as outlined below. For a full discussion of this procedure, see Chapter 1.

    10. Locate the number of the coffee cup graphic on the card that comes with The New Print Shop. The coffee cup is number 10.

    11. Press F2 to bring the graphic selection box on screen.

    12. At the blinking cursor, type 10.

    13. Press ↵.

The word COFFEE is now highlighted in the menu box and the picture of the coffee cup appears in the PREVIEW box as shown in Figure 2.13.

    14. Press ↵ to select the coffee cup graphic.

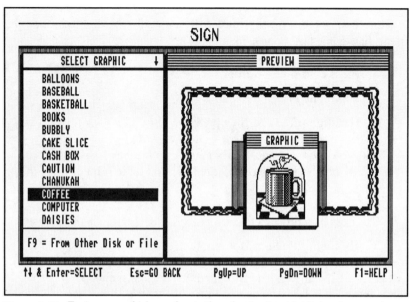

Figure 2.13: Typing a graphic's number in the selection box highlights the name in
the menu box and brings its picture into the PREVIEW box.

Let's move the graphic to the right side of the page to make room for
the price on the left side. To do this, return to the SIGN MENU and
choose the Customize option.

15.   Highlight Customize, then press ↵.

A dialog box now appears asking if you want to save a temporary
copy of your sign. You do not need to save your design before entering
Customize when you haven't created very much yet. If you are just starting a design, you can save time by skipping this step.

16.   Highlight Enter Customize without saving, then press ↵.

The CHOOSE COMMAND menu is now on screen, and a blinking cursor surrounds your sign.

17.   Press ↓ to move the cursor to the coffee cup graphic.

18.   Press M on your keyboard to move the graphic.

19. Press ↑ once to move the cursor away from the border, then press → four times to move it to the side.

20. Press ↵ to choose the cursor position as the new graphic position.

21. Press Esc to return to the SIGN MENU.

Now let's put some words and prices on the sign.

22. Highlight Message, then press ↵.

To be seen from a distance you need a strong, bold font. Choose MADERA in the SOLID style.

23. Highlight MADERA, then press ↵.

24. SOLID is already highlighted, so press ↵ to select it.

25. Press F6 to place the cursor on the left side.

26. Press F5 for large type.

27. Type **Coffee**.

28. Press ↵ to begin a new line.

29. Type **50** in large type.

30. Press ↵ to begin a new line.

31. Press F5 for small size.

32. Type **cents.**

33. Press Esc to return to the SIGN MENU.

Print your sign just the way you printed the certificate.

Stacking Small Signs

Stacked signs (Figure 2.14) are created by taping or gluing together several individual signs.

By using the Small Rows II graphic layout you can create a row of graphics on the top of the first sign and another row on the bottom of the last sign, and then print a long list of items in between.

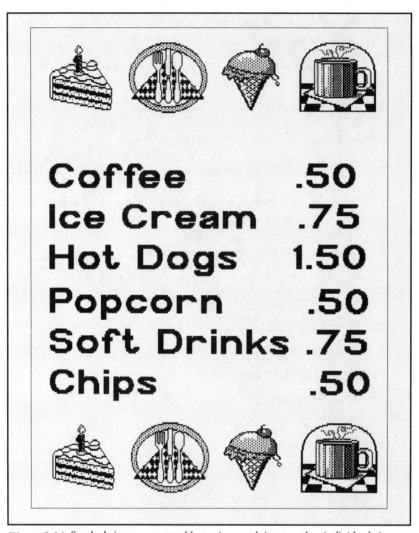

Figure 2.14: Stacked signs are created by taping or gluing together individual signs.

Let's begin this example by performing the first three steps used when you created the previous sign.

1. Once in the SIGN MENU, select Graphic.

2. Next, choose Small Rows II from the SELECT GRAPHIC LAYOUT menu.

3. Select GRAPHICS Hi Res.

4. Highlight CAKE SLICE, then press ⏎.

You now have two rows of cake slices. Let's erase the bottom row.

5. Press ↓ to move the cursor to the first graphic on the bottom.

6. Press the spacebar once to erase it.

7. Repeat this procedure for the other three graphics on the bottom.

Now change some of the graphics to other pictures.

8. Press → twice to highlight the second graphic in the top row.

9. Press C to change the graphic.

10. When the SELECT GRAPHIC menu comes on your screen, press the F2 key to select the graphic by number.

11. Type 27 to select PICNIC PLATE, then press ⏎ twice.

12. Use the same procedure to change the third and fourth graphics on the top line to the ice cream cone graphic (number 18) and the coffee cup graphic (number 10).

13. Press ⏎ to return to the SIGN MENU.

Now add the price list, or message. You will want to use a type that is bold but not too big. Let's choose MADERA.

14. Highlight Message, then press ⏎.

15. Choose MADERA font and SOLID style.

16. Press F6 to align type on the left side of the page.

17. Press ↓ four times to start on the fourth line.

18. Type **Coffee**.

19. Press the spacebar six times, and then type **.50**.

20. Referring to Figure 2.14, type the next two items on the menu, each time using the spacebar enough times to align the price under the one above.

21. Press Esc to return to the SIGN MENU.

Now print the top half of the sign.

To make the bottom half of the sign, erase the graphics from the top line and change them on the bottom line. Then add the rest of the price list on the top of the page. If you want to create a longer price list, print center sheets that list priced items but don't include graphics.

Creating Large Signs and Posters

The New Print Shop has the ability to print in larger sizes for both the tall and wide signs. The first size larger than a single sheet would be 2-by-2 sheets, or across four sheets. (See Figure 2.15 for a diagram of the sizes.) The largest printout uses ten sheets across and ten sheets down, which is about 7-by-9 feet for the tall poster and 9-by-7 feet for the wide version.

How to Use a Full Panel for a Vertical Poster

Let's create a poster for a Thanksgiving Food Drive (Figure 2.16) and print it out in one of the large sizes available. For a food drive for your organization or company, you could print and photocopy small flyers for bulletin boards and make one large poster for a main location.

1. From the MAIN MENU, choose Sign or Poster.

2. Select Design Your Own.

3. Choose Tall from the next menu.

4. Select Graphic from the SIGN MENU.

5. From the SELECT GRAPHIC LAYOUT menu, choose Full Panel.

6. From the list of full panels, choose FOOD.

7. Once you return to the SIGN MENU, select Message.

You will want a big, bold font for this sign.

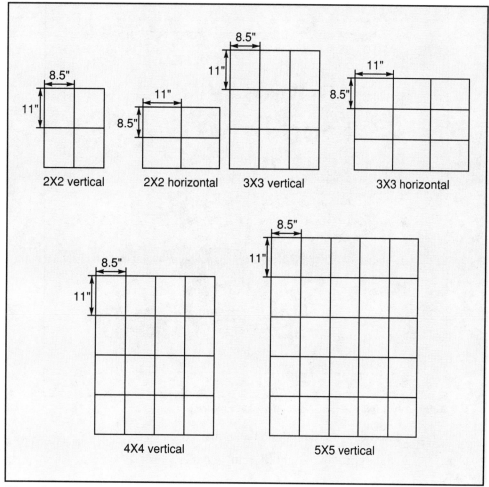

Figure 2.15: Some of the large-size printouts available for the Sign or Poster project

8. Choose AMADOR font and SOLID style.

To get the message for the food drive on this panel, you will need to move the margins. Follow the basic procedure described in Chapter 1, as outlined here:

9. Press the F7 key to begin moving the margins.

10. Highlight Move Left Margin and press ↵.

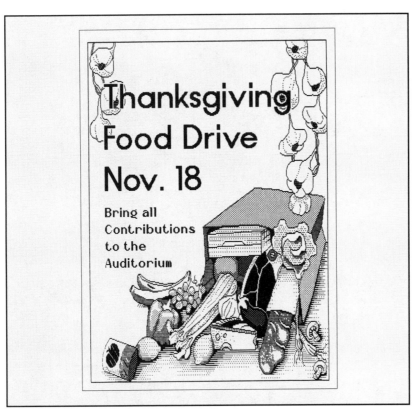

Figure 2.16: Full panels can be used for large posters.

11. Press ← three times, and then press ↵.

12. Highlight Move Right Margin, and then press ↵.

13. Press → three times, and then press ↵.

14. Select Move Bottom Margin.

15. Press ↓ until you reach the bottom of the bananas in the food design, then press ↵.

16. Select Done.

Now you can type the message.

17. Press ↵ to move the cursor to the second line.

18. Press F6 to position the type on the left.

19. Type the following lines, pressing ↵ at the end of each line:

    Thanksgiving

    Food Drive

    Nov. 18

20. On the next line, change the font by pressing F3 and choosing SMALL from the SELECT FONT menu.

As in the certificate example, you won't be able to see the small font in the preview area, but you will be able to view your message in a composition box at the bottom of your screen.

21. Type the following message, pressing ↵ at the end of each line:

    Bring all

    Contributions

    to the

    Auditorium

22. Press Esc to return to the SIGN MENU.

You are now ready to print this poster. Let's choose the 3-by-3 page size. The printer will produce three vertical strips, and you will learn to assemble edge strips and center strips. Any larger size will use the same procedure.

23. Highlight Print or Save on the SIGN MENU, then press ↵.

Printing large sizes can overheat your printer and cause problems. To avoid this you can print in draft quality or set the contrast level lighter on the PRINT OR SAVE MENU. For this example, leave the quality in the default draft mode and change the contrast.

24. Highlight Set Contrast Level, then press ↵.

25. Select the Medium setting.

26. Highlight Select Size from the PRINT OR SAVE MENU, then press ↵.

27. Select the size Three by three.

If you need to test the paper position, do that before beginning to print. Follow the procedure you used when you printed the ready-made card in Chapter 1.

Now you are ready to print. Printing large sizes takes a lot of time. If you have a problem and need to stop printing, you don't have to start over from the beginning. You can begin at the top of a certain strip by selecting that option.

28. Highlight Print on the PRINT OR SAVE MENU, then select Entire Output.

When your printer is finished printing, you will have one long continuous strip of paper. Tear the paper between each three-page section to create three strips.

Notice that the printer has made a slash mark at the top of the first page of each strip and sets of two light dots at intervals down the strip to help you match the sections of the poster. You will need to trim the narrow edge off the left side of the second and third strips. Use the slash mark and the tiny dots as guides. A paper cutter works well here, but cutting by hand through several thicknesses does not. If you are using hand scissors you may want to cut a single page at a time.

Lay the strips out on a hard, flat surface such as a table. Carefully match the design and the guide marks. Although you can use tape to hold the pages together, a glue stick works very well. Hold the strips together firmly with one hand while you lift part of the strip to place the glue. Glue the strips in small sections of about a page at a time. Be careful that the paper doesn't shift.

Now you can hang your sign on a wall or in a window or glue it to cardboard.

Using Color Graphics on Large Signs

The New Print Shop comes with color graphics that you can use if you have a color printer. The birthday cake shown in Figure 2.17 is one of these.

Figure 2.17: The birthday cake is one of the color graphics that come with The New Print Shop. It can be converted for black-and-white use with the Convert feature in the new program.

You can convert the color graphics for black-and-white use with the Convert feature in The New Print Shop. For instructions on how to do this, see the section on converting color graphics in Chapter 10.

To create the birthday cake sign in Figure 2.17:

1. Once inside Sign or Poster project, choose Design Your Own, and then select the Wide sign option.

2. Select Border from the SIGN MENU.

3. Choose THIN BORDER, and then select NEON.

4. From the SELECT GRAPHIC LAYOUT menu, choose Medium Bottom.

On the next menu, GRAPHICS Hi Res is highlighted. You do not want this file this time. If you are set up with a color printer, the file that contains the multicolor graphics is also listed. If you are not set up with a color printer, you cannot access the multicolor files.

5. Highlight the color file, then press ↵.

The menu for the color graphics should be in the menu box.

6. Highlight Birthday, then press ↵

You will need to go into Customize to move the cake to the lower-right corner.

7. Highlight Customize and press ↵.
8. Press ↑ and → several times to position the graphic as shown in Figure 2.17.
9. Select the AMADOR font and SOLID style.
10. Press F6 to align the cursor on the left side of the page.
11. Press the spacebar once to start the message away from the border and type **Party**.
12. Press ↵.
13. Press the spacebar once and type **Cakes**.
14. Press ↵.
15. Press F3 to change fonts and choose SMALL.
16. Type the following lines, adding a space at the beginning of each line and pressing ↵ at the end of each line:

> **Sheet**
>
> **Half Sheet**
>
> **Round**
>
> **Layered**

17. Press Esc to return to the SIGN MENU.

You can print your large sign using the same procedure as you did for the Thanksgiving poster. Assembling the horizontal sign will be a little different, because you will have horizontal strips instead of vertical ones. Just trim the narrow edge and match the guide marks.

Creating Scenery for Skits and Plays

Some of the full panels and small graphics can be used as stage scenery for skits and plays when printed out in one of the larger sizes.

A full panel, such as the one in Figure 2.18, can be used as it is. You might want to print it out in a light contrast and color it in with paints. This village scene is one of the panels available in the Sampler Edition Graphics Library, a separate program available from Brøderbund to use with The New Print Shop.

Small graphics such as the sunshine graphic (Figure 2.19) can also be used in creating backdrops. These, too, can be printed out in light contrast and colored. Small graphics need a little adjusting before printing. They must first fill a whole page so that they print out correctly in the size.

Figure 2.18: Full panels, such as this one from the Sampler Edition Graphics Library, can be used for large-size printing.

In the next example, you'll prepare a window for a skit using the sunshine graphic.

1. Once in the Sign or Poster project, select Design Your Own, then select the Tall option.

2. From the SIGN MENU, choose Graphic.

3. From the SELECT GRAPHIC LAYOUT menu, choose Large Top.

4. Select GRAPHICS Hi Res, then select SUNSHINE from the list of graphics.

5. Press ⏎ to return to the SIGN MENU.

Figure 2.19: With a little adjusting in Customize, small graphics can be used to make backdrops, too.

6. Enter Customize to move and stretch the graphic.

7. Press M, then press ↑ to move the cursor to the top as far as it will go.

8. Press ← to move the cursor to the left as far as it will go.

9. Press ↵ to move the graphic to the cursor's new position.

10. Press S, then press → several times to stretch the cursor all the way across the design area.

11. Press ↓ several times to stretch the cursor to the bottom of the design area.

12. Press ↵ to stretch the graphic to fit the new cursor area.

You should now have a graphic that fills the page. It is ready to be printed out; just choose one of the large sizes available in the Select Size option from the PRINT OR SAVE MENU.

Printing Backwards for Heat-Transfer Designs

The Sign or Poster project can be used to create designs to iron on T-shirts and sweatshirts. To create an iron-on design such as the one in Figure 2.20, use the Sign or Poster project to create the graphic and message you want to use. Put a heat-transfer ribbon in your printer and use the Print Backwards feature to create a reverse image. Following the instructions that come with your heat-transfer ribbon or those given in Chapter 14, iron the design onto T-shirts, sweatshirts, or any fabric.

To create the design in Figure 2.20:

1. Once in the Sign or Poster project, select Design Your Own, then choose the Tall option.

2. Choose Graphic from the SIGN MENU.

3. From the SELECT GRAPHICS LAYOUT menu, choose Large Centered.

Figure 2.20: In the Sign or Poster project, you can create designs for T-shirts and sweatshirts.

4. Select GRAPHICS Hi Res, then choose RIBBON from the list of graphics.

5. Once back in the SIGN MENU, highlight Message, and then press ↵.

6. Select SIERRA font in the SOLID style.

7. Press F5 to make the type large, then type **State** above the graphic. (Don't worry about the word being too high above the graphic; you will move it using the Customize option later.)

8. Type **Champion** in large type below the ribbon.

9. Position the cursor over the center of the ribbon.

10. Press F3 to change fonts, and choose SMALL.

11. Press F6 to align the cursor on the left.

12. Press the spacebar until the cursor is near the center of the ribbon.

13. Type **1st**. (This line will be too high on the graphic, and you will have to stretch it to fit in Customize.)

14. Press Esc to return to the SIGN MENU.

15. Highlight Customize, then press ↵.

16. Press ↵ to save a temporary copy of your design when the dialog box appears.

17. Highlight **State**.

18. Press T to change this text to a graphic, then choose Convert Text to Graphic.

19. Press M to move it.

20. Press ↓ twice, then press ↵ to move the word to the new cursor position.

21. Highlight **1st**.

22. Press S to stretch this line.

23. Press ↓ once, then press ↵ to stretch the line to fit into the larger cursor area.

24. Press Esc to return to the SIGN MENU.

Print your design, setting the print quality to Enhanced Final Quality and choosing Print Backwards from the PRINT OR SAVE MENU. Remember to put a heat-transfer ribbon into your printer.

If you want to color your design with fabric paint or pens, you might want to use the Outline font style for the message. You can also create an outline effect for the graphic. Figure 2.21 shows the same heat-transfer design in the outline style.

Try these steps to change the ribbon in the current example to an outlined graphic:

1. Enter Customize from the SIGN MENU.

2. Highlight the ribbon graphic.

3. Press G to change the style of the graphic.

4. Choose OUTLINE from the next menu.

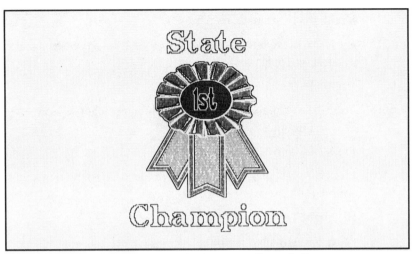

*Figure 2.21: You can create the same design in an outline style if you want to use
fabric paint or pens to color it.*

Exploring Other Options

Most of the examples you have tried so far in the Sign or Poster
project have been designed to hang on a window or wall. But you are not
limited to making only signs and posters with this project, as you will
see in the following sections. Use the ideas presented in the rest of this
chapter as a springboard to designing your own creations with the Sign
or Poster project.

Creating Covers

With The New Print Shop, you can create a report cover or a program
cover using all of the features of the Sign or Poster project.

Creating Formal Report Covers

Students and business people have used the original Print Shop to create exciting report covers. Some of the features in The New Print Shop
allow you to create even more interesting ones.

The report cover in Figure 2.22 was created using the Small Tiled
graphic layout pattern and erasing a center section for the report title.

Figure 2.22: You can create formal report covers by choosing the Small Tiled graphic layout and erasing a center area for the title.

Try creating this cover yourself:

1. Once in the Sign or Poster project, choose Design Your Own.

2. Choose the Tall poster option from the next menu.

3. When the SIGN MENU appears, select Graphic.

4. Choose Small Tiled for the graphic layout.

5. Choose PATTERNS Original from the next menu, then select SHAPES.

6. Move the cursor to the second tile in the second row.

7. Press the spacebar to erase it.

8.   Erase the next two tiles to the right using the same method.

9.   Erase the three center tiles in the next two rows.

10.   Press ↵ to accept the changes in the graphic layout.

11.   Highlight Message on the SIGN MENU, then press ↵.

12.   Choose SIERRA font in the SOLID style.

13.   Press ↓ three times to move the cursor inside the blank box you've created.

14.   Type the following message, pressing ↵ at the end of each line:

Carnival

Committee

Report

1992

15.   Press Esc to return to the SIGN MENU.

An Example of an Informal Report Cover

A more informal style of report cover (Figure 2.23) can be created selecting the Medium Staggered graphic layout, erasing the center graphic and changing the other graphics.

Using Two Sizes of Graphics

An important new feature in The New Print Shop is the ability to put more than one size graphic on a page. Let's create the report cover shown in Figure 2.24 to demonstrate one way to do this.

1.   Once in the Sign or Poster project, select Design Your Own, then choose the Tall sign option.

2.   From the SIGN MENU, choose Graphic.

3.   Choose Small Frame for the graphic layout.

4.   Choose GRAPHICS Hi Res.

5.   Press F2 to select the music graphic by number.

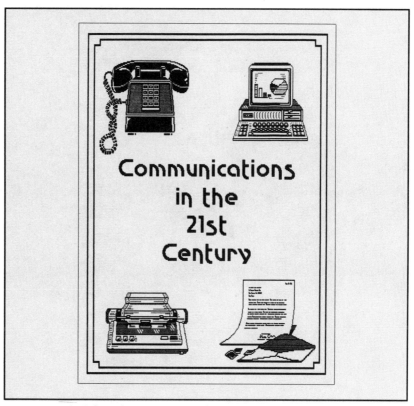

Figure 2.23: An informal report cover can be created by using the Medium Staggered graphic layout.

6. When prompted, type 22, the number for the music graphic.

7. Press ↵ three times to return to the SIGN MENU.

8. Highlight Customize, and then press ↵.

9. Press I to insert a graphic.

You will be asked to select a size for the graphic you want to insert. You can choose to insert a small, medium, or large graphic.

10. Choose Medium Graphic.

11. Choose GRAPHICS Hi Res.

12. Press F2 to select the piano graphic by number.

Figure 2.24: An important new feature in The New Print Shop is the ability to use more than one size graphic on a page.

13. When prompted, type 26, the number for the piano graphic.

14. Press ↵ twice.

A blinking cursor box appears in the upper-left corner of your screen. You must move it with the arrow keys to the position where you wish to place your piano graphic.

15. Press ↓ seven times and → nine times to position the blinking cursor box close to the center of the design.

16. Press ↵ to insert the piano.

17. Press ↓ until the piano is highlighted by the blinking cursor box.

18. Press A to align the graphic and choose Vertically Centered from the following menu.

19. Press Esc to return to the SIGN MENU.

20. Highlight Message, then press ↵.

21. Choose SIERRA font in SOLID style.

22. Press ↵ twice to move the cursor to a line just above the piano.

23. Type **Piano**.

24. Press ↵ five times to move cursor to line just below the piano.

25. Type **Music**.

26. Preview the cover by pressing F10.

27. Press any key to continue.

28. Press Esc to return to the SIGN MENU.

You may now print your cover.

Designing a Program Cover

A cover for an 8½-by-5½-inch program can be created with The New Print Shop. Put the design you want on the front of the program on the right side of a wide sign. Then fold the printed page in half to create the cover.

Figure 2.25 shows a program cover for a Christmas concert by the community choir. It uses a thin border of evergreen trees from the Party Edition of The New Print Shop Graphics Library. The SMALL font in the OUTLINE style is used for the words **Christmas Concert** and the TINY font in the SOLID style for the rest of the cover.

You can use a thin or wide border for the program cover or no border at all. Choose the SMALL or TINY font to get type small enough to fit on one side of the page.

Using a Graphic by Itself

You can use only the graphics part of the Sign or Poster project to create additional products.

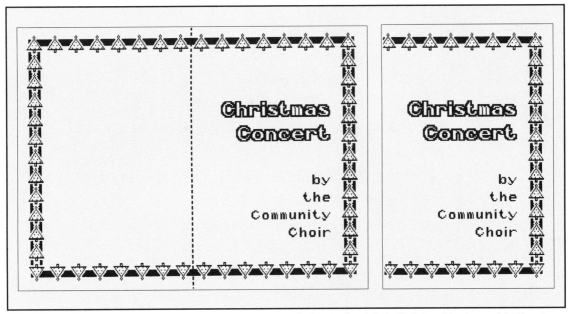

Figure 2.25: A program cover can be created by putting your design on the right half of the wide sign and folding the paper in half.

Creating Large Cutouts

Perhaps you need a large graphic for a bulletin board display or a wall or window decoration. Using the same technique that you used to create the window for the stage scenery, you can enlarge any graphic to page size, then print it out in that size or a larger size.

The teddy bear graphic (Figure 2.26) was printed page size and then printed backwards. Both were later cut out and pasted back to back to create a window display that could be seen from both sides of the window. A similar two-sided graphic could be hung in a mobile decoration.

Creating Decorative Papers

By printing a graphic in the Small Tiled layout, you can produce decorative, patterned papers. Figure 2.27 shows an example.

By erasing some of the graphics in the Small Tiled layout or changing a few of them, you can create other interesting effects, as shown in Figure 2.28.

Figure 2.26: By printing a page-size graphic in both standard and backwards printing, you can create a front and back.

By printing in colored ribbon on colored paper you can produce a product that can be used for many crafts. For more information on printing ideas, see Chapter 14.

Using a Border by Itself

You can use a border by itself, especially one of the wide borders, for many products.

A page-size printout can make a nice small place mat. The 2-by-2 sheet size makes an ideal place mat for use under a centerpiece or table decoration.

By printing out a page with a border and cutting out its center, you can create a frame to be used around a drawing, photograph, or word processed printout. You can also print an oversized frame for larger pieces. This is a good and inexpensive way to frame children's artwork.

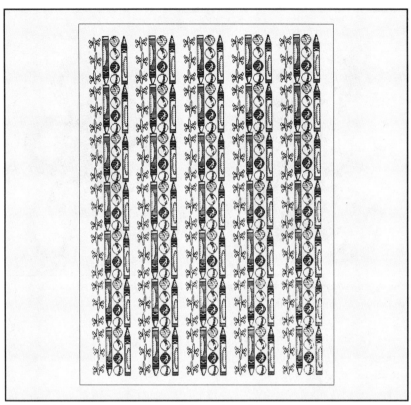

Figure 2.27: You can create an overall design for a decorative paper by using a small graphic in the Small Tiled layout.

Using a Message by Itself

While the message is usually the most important part of the sign, graphics and a border help convey the message. Sometimes, however, words alone are best.

Select Your Words Carefully

When you are using only words, it is very important to select them carefully. Too many words can make a sign difficult to read and hard to understand. Use only the words you need.

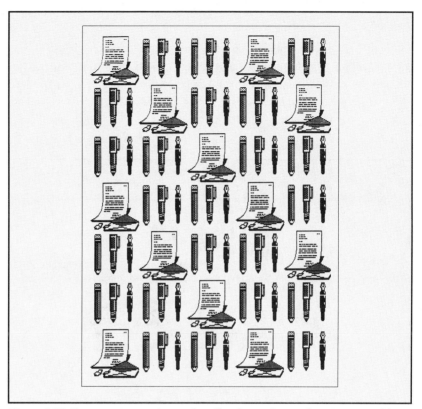

Figure 2.28: You can create an interesting effect by erasing or changing some of the graphics in the Small Tiled layout.

You may want to tell your customers that "This door is broken, please use the other one." But the sign you put on the door should merely say, "Use Other Door."

Use Size and Style for Emphasis

While long messages are difficult to read, signs in all one size and type are also difficult to read. Give some thought to which words are most important in your message and put those in larger type.

If you really want to emphasize a word or two, use one of the special styles.

Figure 2.29 shows how a simple sign with only a few words can convey a message effectively.

Use Fonts Effectively

Each font has characteristics that can add to your message. Some signs need a big, bold type that can be read across the room. Some signs need a rustic look, others, a formal appearance. Some need a modern type while others need a flowing script. Be sure that the font you use matches your message.

Figure 2.29: When a sign needs only words, you can change typesize or style for emphasis and easy reading.

3 *Creating Letterheads*

With the Letterhead project you can create interesting letterheads for your personal stationery, business letters, and memos. You can also use it to print large-size banners with full panel graphics or small graphics in the center of the banner. The Letterhead project allows you to create an interesting top and bottom for your personal or business stationery.

You can use any of the graphics and fonts that come with The New Print Shop to create your own design, or you can start with one of the full panels and then add more text or graphics.

All of the customizing features are available to use in designing the letterhead.

The procedure for designing both top and bottom sections of your stationery is the same. As with all the projects, you can watch your creation take shape in the PREVIEW box.

The letterheads you create with this project can be printed up to ten times larger than the standard 8½-by-11-inch size and one or two pages deep. Such a banner can utilize all the Letterhead layouts and graphics, allowing you to create a banner that prints a full panel design across many pages. The banners made with the Letterhead project are printed horizontally across the pages, which means that you must assemble the individual pages to make the banner.

To understand the opportunities available in this project, let's create a few sample letterheads. You'll learn how to create a personal letterhead for individual use, a business letterhead that helps promote a small business, and an organization letterhead for a club or community group.

In the additional options section, you will discover other uses for letterheads, such as memos, menus, and sign-up sheets. You'll also learn how to create banners that use full panel graphics and graphic layouts.

The program comes with four ready-made letterheads to start you off with a few ideas.

Designing Your Own Letterheads

To learn how to make letterheads and discover many of the opportunities for creativity in The New Print Shop program, let's create some samples.

Creating a Letterhead for Personal Use

Begin by creating the personal letterhead for Sam Jones, as shown in Figure 3.1.

Enter the Letterhead project.

1. Highlight Letterhead on the MAIN MENU as shown in Figure 3.2, then press ↵.

The first LETTERHEAD screen is similar to the ones you used in the Greeting Card and Sign or Poster projects. A menu appears on the left of the screen. Press ↑ or ↓ to highlight your selections. The message below the menu changes as you highlight each choice. You can watch

Figure 3.1:Many personal letterheads use only the top section of the Letterhead project.

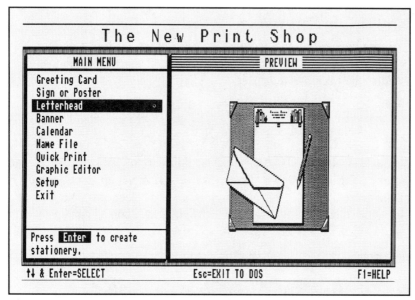

Figure 3.2: To use the Letterhead project, highlight Letterhead on the MAIN MENU.

your design as you create it in the PREVIEW box. Across the bottom of the screen an information box offers extra help.

This screen allows you to choose one of these options:

Design Your Own

Use a Ready Made

Load a Saved Letterhead

Design Your Own is already highlighted.

2. Press ↵ to select Design Your Own.

The next screen that appears is the LETTERHEAD: Top screen (Figure 3.3).

The TOP MENU on the LETTERHEAD: Top screen allows you to choose these options:

Graphic

Text

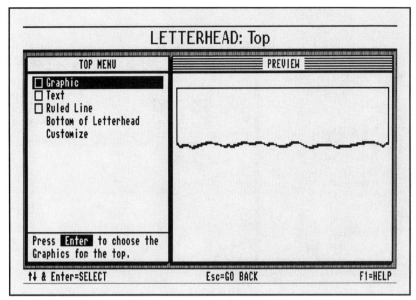

Figure 3.3: *The LETTERHEAD: Top screen allows you to create the top of your letterhead.*

Ruled Line

Bottom of Letterhead

Customize

Graphic is already highlighted.

3. Press ↵ to select Graphic.

The SELECT GRAPHIC LAYOUT menu now appears (Figure 3.4). The menu lets you choose the layout for the graphics for the top of the letterhead. You will notice that there are no choices for large graphics on this menu—only small and medium graphics are available in the Letterhead project.

4. Press ↓ eight times to highlight Medium Ends, then press ↵.

The next menu allows you to select the file that holds the graphics you wish to use. GRAPHICS Hi Res is already highlighted.

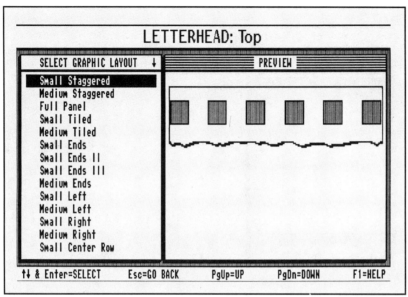

Figure 3.4: This SELECT GRAPHIC LAYOUT menu lets you choose a layout for the top of the letterhead.

5. Press ↵ to select GRAPHICS Hi Res.

The menu on the next screen, **SELECT GRAPHIC**, offers the same choices available in the Greeting Card and Sign projects. The arrow next to the menu title indicates there are more graphics listed than those now on-screen.

6. Highlight DESERT, then press ↵ to select it.

You could change one of the graphics or the layout now, but we'll do that later.

7. Press ↵ to accept this graphic and this layout.

When you return to the LETTERHEAD: Top screen, Text should be highlighted.

8. Press ↵ to select Text.

The SELECT FONT menu that appears now is the same as the font selection screens you used in the Greeting Card and Sign projects.

9. Press ↓ seven times to highlight the SONOMA font, then press ↵.

The SELECT STYLE menu is also the same as that used for the other projects. SOLID is already highlighted.

10. Press ↵ to select SOLID.

The EDIT COMMANDS menu now appears, listing the commands that you can use to create your text. The font and style that you are currently using are listed below the menu. You can change the font and style on every line. However, the program is set up to use your current choice of font on the top line and then drops to TINY font for the next lines. Let's create some text to see how the program is set up.

11. Type **Sam Jones** on the first line.

12. Press ↵ to begin a new line.

The size of the cursor has now changed and the font listed below the menu is now TINY.

As you will see in the following steps, when type is too small to see in the preview area, it appears in a composition box at the bottom of the screen.

13. Type **Southwest Regional Director** on this line.

14. Press ↵ to begin a new line.

15. Type **2270 Highway 75**.

16. Press ↵ to begin a new line.

17. Type **Desert, Arizona 00900**.

18. Press the F8 key to center the text top to bottom.

19. Press the F10 key to preview your design.

20. Press any key to continue.

21. Press Esc to return to the LETTERHEAD: Top screen.

When you return to the LETTERHEAD: Top screen, Ruled Line is now highlighted.

22. Press ↵ to select Ruled Line.

23. Highlight Thick Line, then press ↵.

You are now ready to proceed to the bottom of the letterhead.

24. Once you return to the TOP MENU, highlight Bottom of Letterhead, then press ↵.

The LETTERHEAD: Bottom screen now appears (Figure 3.5). It is the same as the LETTERHEAD: Top screen except for the Print or Save menu option.

Since you will not create a bottom for this example, go directly to the PRINT OR SAVE MENU.

25. Highlight Print or Save, then press ↵.

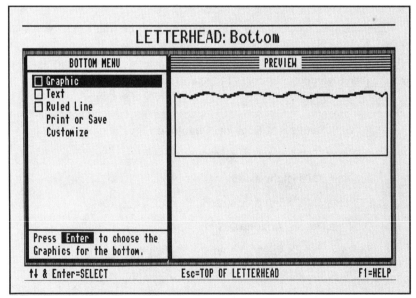

Figure 3.5: The LETTERHEAD: Bottom screen is almost the same as the top one except for the Print or Save choice.

The PRINT OR SAVE MENU for the Letterhead project is almost the same as the one used for the Sign project except that there is no backward print option on the Letterhead Print menu and the size menus of the two projects offer very different sizes.

To print out your letterhead, use the same procedure as you used to print signs.

26. Set the print quality to Enhanced Final Quality.

27. Test the paper position to be sure you will start on the first line.

28. Print the letterhead.

29. Save the letterhead.

30. Exit to the MAIN MENU.

Creating a Letterhead for a Small Business

The New Print Shop can create some nice letterheads for small businesses. Not only are they inexpensive letterheads, they can also be easily changed, allowing you to include special promotions or seasonal messages in the bottom area.

Let's continue exploring the Letterhead project by creating the sample letterhead for Cathy's Catering Service as shown in Figure 3.6.

Once in the Letterhead project, select Design Your Own. The LETTERHEAD: Top screen now appears. The Graphic option is highlighted.

1. Press ↵ to select Graphics.

2. Highlight Small Ends II, then press ↵.

3. Press ↵ again to choose GRAPHICS Hi Res.

4. Highlight the CAKE SLICE graphic, then press ↵.

5. Press ↵ again to return to the LETTERHEAD: Top screen.

Both of the cake graphics will be facing the same way now, but you can change them later.

When you return to the LETTERHEAD: Top screen, the Text option will be highlighted.

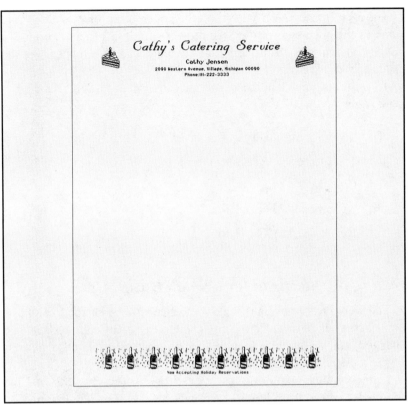

Figure 3.6: This letterhead for Cathy's Catering Service uses small graphics on the top and seasonal promotion messages on the bottom.

6. Press ↵ to select Text.

7. Highlight MERCED from the SELECT FONT menu, and press ↵.

8. Highlight SOLID from the SELECT STYLE menu, and press ↵.

9. Type **Cathy's Catering Service** and press ↵ to begin a new line.

The program now automatically switches to the TINY font, as you can see by the small cursor and the font listing below the menu. Cathy's name should be in a slightly larger type than the address. Let's change the font.

10. Press F3 to change the font.

11. Highlight SMALL, then press ↵.

12. Type **Cathy Jensen**.

13. Press ↵ to begin a new line.

The font has changed back to TINY. Type the address and phone number in this font on the next two lines.

14. Type **2090 Western Avenue, Village, Michigan 00090**.

15. Press ↵ to begin a new line.

16. Type **Phone: 111-222-3333**.

17. Press F8 to center the text top to bottom.

18. Press F10 to preview your work.

19. Press any key to continue.

20. Press Esc to return to the LETTERHEAD: Top screen.

Now it's time to turn that cake slice around and make a few other adjustments. The ability to make these adjustments is one of the best features of The New Print Shop program.

Graphics should always face the center of the page. This attracts the reader's eye to the page and your message. Flip the right graphic with the Customize option.

21. Highlight Customize, then press ↵.

When the dialog box appears and asks if you want to save a temporary copy of your work, do so. If you are not happy with the changes you make in Customize, you can return to this version by choosing Restore from the CHOOSE COMMAND menu.

22. Press ↵ to save a temporary copy of your design.

When you enter Customize, the blinking cursor box highlights the left cake slice. You want to move it to the right one.

23. Press → to highlight the right cake slice.

24. Press F to flip the graphic.

25. Press H to get a horizontal mirror image of the graphic.

You need to make a few more adjustments. The cake slices are far away from the text. Let's bring them closer so they become a part of the whole design.

26. While the blinking cursor is still on the right cake slice, press M to move it.

27. Press ← four times to move the cursor closer to the text.

28. Press ↵ to move the graphic to the new cursor position.

29. Press ← once to highlight the left cake slice.

30. Press M to move it.

31. Press → four times to move the cursor closer to the text.

32. Press ↵ to move the graphic to the new cursor position.

33. Press Esc to return to the LETTERHEAD: Top screen.

Now you are ready to create the bottom of this letterhead.

34. Highlight Bottom of Letterhead on the TOP MENU, then press ↵.

35. Highlight Graphic on the BOTTOM MENU, then press ↵.

Cathy's Catering Service letterhead uses the bottom section to remind readers that Cathy is already accepting reservations for Christmas and New Year's Eve parties.

36. Highlight Small Center Row, then press ↵.

37. Since GRAPHIC Hi Res is already highlighted, press ↵ to select it.

38. Highlight BUBBLY, then press ↵ twice to select the graphic and return to the LETTERHEAD: Bottom screen.

The Text selection is highlighted on the menu. You will need to create one line of text below the bottles.

39. Press ↵ to select Text.

40. Highlight TINY, then press ↵.

41. Highlight SOLID and press ↵.

42. Press ↓ six times to place the cursor below the graphic.

43. Type **Now Accepting Holiday Reservations**.

44. Press Esc to return to the LETTERHEAD: Bottom screen.

You can now proceed to the PRINT OR SAVE MENU and print out the letterhead.

Creating a Letterhead for Your Club or Organization

Members of clubs and organizations can now create attractive letterheads for their groups with The New Print Shop. The example in Figure 3.7 uses one of the full panels that comes with the program. Let's create this sample to explore additional features of the Letterhead project.

1. Choose the Letterhead project from the MAIN MENU.

2. Highlight Design Your Own and press ↵.

3. Highlight Graphic and press ↵.

4. Highlight Full Panel, then press ↵.

The CHOOSE FULL PANEL menu lists all the panels that are available for use with the Letterhead project. With the F10 key you can preview any full panel on the list to help you select the one you want (Figure 3.8).

5. Press ↓ to highlight IRISES, and then press ↵.

6. Press F10 to preview the IRISES full panel.

7. Press any key to continue.

8. Press ↵ to select the IRISES full panel.

You can put the text you need onto the full panel graphic. Text is already highlighted.

9. Press ↵ to select Text.

10. From the SELECT FONT menu, select SONOMA.

11. From the SELECT STYLE menu, choose SOLID.

Note the position of the left and right margin tabs on screen. As you can see, the name of the garden club will not fit in this space unless you change the margins. Change them before you type the text.

12. Press F7 to change the margins.

Figure 3.7: Full panel graphics available with The New Print Shop provide attractive letterheads for clubs and organizations.

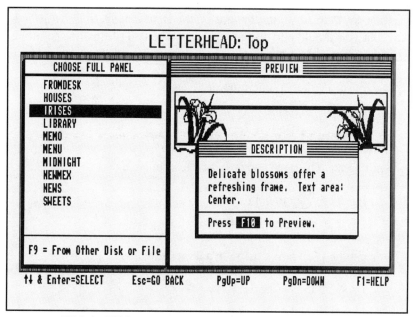

Figure 3.8: With the F10 key you can preview any selection from the full panel menu.

13. Highlight Move Left Margin, then press ↵.

14. Press ← twice to move the cursor.

15. Press ↵ to accept the current cursor position as the new left margin.

16. Highlight Move Right Margin, then press ↵.

17. Press the → key twice to move the cursor.

18. Press ↵ to accept the current cursor position as the new right margin.

19. Highlight Done, then press ↵.

20. Type **West Side Garden Club**.

Preview the design to see how the typed line fits in the panel. It's a good idea to check your progress often.

21. Press F10 to preview your work.

The word **Club** runs into the leaf on the right side. A little overlap is okay, but you should add a space or two at the end of this line to move the name to the left a little.

22. Press any key to continue.

23. Press the spacebar once to add a space to the end of the line.

24. Press the F10 key to preview your work again.

That's better. The **b** in **Club** won't be lost in the leaf.

25. Press any key to continue.

26. Press ↵ to begin a new line.

Let's put the president's name in a larger font.

27. Press F3 to change the font.

28. Highlight SMALL and press ↵.

29. Type **Nancy Smith, President.**

30. Press ↵ to begin a new line.

31. Type the address on the next two lines in the default type, TINY.

2034 North Street

Southville, Indiana 11111

32. Press F10 to preview your work.

33. Press Esc to return to the LETTERHEAD: Top screen.

You've finished the top of the letterhead and are ready to create the bottom.

34. Highlight Bottom of Letterhead and press ↵.

Let's begin by choosing a double line that will match the line surrounding the top border.

35. Highlight Ruled Line and press ↵.

36. Highlight Double Line and press ↵.

Now create the text. The first line of text is preset in the SMALL font and the additional lines in TINY. To use the SMALL font for all the officers' names, you will need to change the font for each line.

37. Highlight Text and press ↵.

38. Highlight SMALL, then press ↵.

39. SOLID is highlighted. Press ↵ to select it.

40. Type **Vice President, Claude Nelson.**

41. Press F10 to preview this line.

The line looks as if it will print over the border. We will fix this later when we center the text top to bottom.

42. Press ↵ to begin a new line.

43. Press F3 and choose the SMALL font again.

44. Type **Treasurer, Alicia Brandenberg.**

45. Press ↵ to begin a new line.

46. Press F3 and choose SMALL font before typing each of the following lines.

    Secretary, Marge Morehead

    Program Chairman, Ted Martinez

    Publicity, Rhonda Stearns

47. With the cursor on the last line after **Stearns**, press F8 to center your message top to bottom.

48. Press F10 to preview your work.

49. Press any key to continue.

50. Press Esc to return to the LETTERHEAD: Bottom screen.

51. Print and save your work.

*E*xploring Other Options

Any memo, menu, or sign-up sheet that needs a fancy heading can be created with the Letterhead project. The following section shows you how to create these items and also demonstrates additional features of the Letterhead project.

*C*reating Memos, Menus, and Other Notes

When you created the letterheads in the above examples, you left the center part of the page blank to create a letter with a typewriter or word processor. But the center does not have to contain a letter. It could be a memo or menu or any other note. You could type a menu letterhead, such as the one in Figure 3.9. The menu could be typed or pasted in the center area and then photocopied for additional copies.

Let's create this example to explore other special features of the Letterhead project.

1. Once in the Letterhead project, choose Design Your Own.

2. From the TOP MENU, select Graphic.

3. From the SELECT GRAPHIC LAYOUT screen, choose Medium Right.

4. Choose GRAPHIC Hi Res, then press ↵.

5. Press F2 to select the graphic by number.

6. Since the PICNIC graphic's number is 27, type 27.

7. Press ↵ to select the graphic and twice more to return to the LETTERHEAD: Top screen.

You can now create the text for the top of this menu.

8. Highlight Text and press ↵.

9. Choose the AMADOR font and the 3-D style.

10. Press F6 to align the type on the left side of the page.

Figure 3.9: With the Letterhead project you can create a menu for daily lunch specials.

Just as in the organization letterhead, you can use blank spaces to position your text.

11. Press the spacebar three times before typing **Wednesday**.

12. Press ↵ to begin a new line.

13. Press F3 and choose the AMADOR font again for the next line.

14. Press F6 twice to center this line.

15. Type **Lunch Specials**.

16. Press F8 to center the type top to bottom.

17. Press the F10 key to preview your work.

18. Press any key to continue.

19. Press Esc to return to the LETTERHEAD: Top screen.

Let's choose a thick line to set this heading apart from the menu area.

20. Highlight Ruled Line and press ↵.

21. Choose Thick Line and press ↵.

The picnic graphic is a little too far to the right. Let's try changing it with Customize.

22. Highlight Customize and press ↵.

23. When the dialog box appears, save a temporary copy of the letterhead.

24. Press ↑ to highlight the picnic graphic.

25. Press M to move the graphic.

A blinking cursor now appears around the graphic.

26. Press ← three times to move the cursor.

27. Press ↵ to move the graphic to the new cursor position.

28. Press Esc to return to the LETTERHEAD: Top screen.

That looks better. Now you'll create the bottom.

29. Highlight Bottom of Letterhead and press ↵.

30. Highlight Graphic and press ↵.

31. Highlight Small Staggered II, then press ↵.

32. Choose GRAPHICS Hi Res and press ↵.

33. Press F2 to select the graphic by number.

34. Type 18 for the ICE CREAM graphic and press ↵ twice to select it.

35. Press → to highlight the 2nd cone.

36. Press the spacebar to erase it.

37. Erase the 3rd, 5th, 6th, 8th, and 9th cones the same way.

38. Press ↵ to return to the LETTERHEAD: Bottom screen.

You will now use some special features to create the text for the bottom. First you will create one section, center it, and then clone it to create the other two sections. Then you will add the bottom line.

39. Highlight Text and press ↵.

40. Choose SMALL font in SOLID style.

41. Type **FREE**.

42. Type the next two lines in TINY font.

    Ice

    Cream

43. Press F8 to center the type top to bottom.

44. Preview your design.

45. Press any key to continue.

46. Press Esc to return to the LETTERHEAD: Bottom screen.

Let's place a thin ruled line in this bottom design to hold it together and separate it from the menu area.

47. Highlight Ruled Line, then press ↵.

48. Highlight Thin, then press ↵.

Now you need to go into Customize to copy, or clone, the type.

49. Highlight Customize and press ↵.

50. When the dialog box appears, save a temporary copy of your design.

51. Highlight **FREE**.

52. Press T to change the text to a graphic, then choose Convert the Text to Graphic when the dialog box appears.

53. Press C to clone **FREE**.

54. Press → 18 times to move the cursor to the middle of the space on the right.

55. Press ↵ to copy **FREE** to the new cursor position.

56. Press C again, and then press ← 18 times to move the cursor to the middle of the space on the left.

57. Press ↵ to clone **FREE** to the new cursor position.

58. Clone the next two lines the same way on both the right and the left side.

59. Press Esc to return to the LETTERHEAD: Bottom screen.

Now add the last line of text. If you tried to enter it when you placed the other text in the bottom section, you would have disturbed the centering for those lines. Now that the other text has been changed to a graphic, you can add this text without affecting the placement of the first words.

60. Highlight Text, then press ↵.

61. Select TINY font and SOLID style.

62. Press ↓ six times to place the cursor below the graphics.

63. Type **With Every Lunch**.

64. Press Esc to return to the LETTERHEAD: Bottom screen.

Let's go back into Customize and stretch this line of text to make it bigger.

65. Highlight Customize, then press ↵.

66. Save a temporary copy of the menu.

67. Highlight the new line of text.

68. Press T and select Convert the Text to Graphic to change the text to a graphic.

69. Press S to stretch the text.

70. Press → five times and ↓ once to stretch the cursor.

71. Press ↵ to stretch the text to fit the cursor.

72. Press A to align the text and H to center it horizontally.

73. Press Esc to return to the BOTTOM MENU.

74. Print and save the menu.

Creating Sign-Up Sheets

Many times when you attend a meeting, officers or committee chairmen will pass around a sign-up sheet and ask people to volunteer for one thing or another. Sometimes more than one sheet will be passed around.

With attractive headings and informative bottoms created in The New Print Shop, volunteers will never be confused about which sign-up sheet they are signing or what is expected of them (see Figure 3.10).

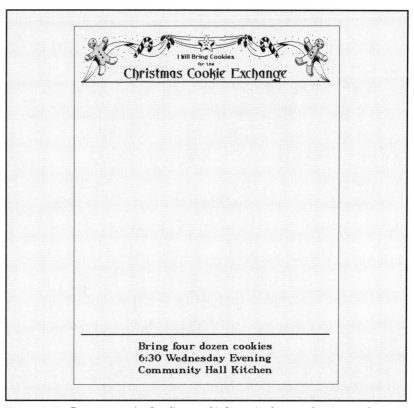

Figure 3.10: Create attractive headings and informative bottoms for sign-up sheets.

The example in Figure 3.10 begins with a full panel. Enter SELECT GRAPHIC LAYOUT for the top of the sign-up sheet the same way you did at the beginning of the previous example.

1. From the SELECT GRAPHIC LAYOUT menu, choose Full Panel.

2. Select SWEETS.

3. Select Text from the TOP MENU.

4. Choose the SMALL font in the SOLID style.

5. Press ↵ or ↓ to move the cursor down one line. Note that the font has changed to TINY.

6. Press F3 to change fonts, then select SMALL.

7. Type **I Will Bring Cookies.**

8. Press ↵ to begin the next line.

9. When you begin the next line, the font changes to TINY again. Type **for the** in this font.

10. Press ↵ to begin the next line.

11. Press F3 to change fonts and choose VENTURA type.

12. Type **Christmas Cookie Exchange.**

13. Preview your design.

14. Press any key to continue.

15. Press Esc to return to the LETTERHEAD: Top screen.

16. Select Ruled Line, then choose Thick Line from the next menu.

17. Proceed to the bottom of the letterhead.

18. Select Ruled Line, then Thick Line.

19. Highlight Text from the BOTTOM MENU and press ↵ to select it.

20. Choose SIERRA font in SOLID style.

Because the Letterhead bottom automatically uses the TINY font, you will need to select SIERRA for each line.

21. Type the following three lines, changing the font to SIERRA for each line:

> **Bring four dozen cookies**
>
> **6:30 Wednesday Evening**
>
> **Community Hall Kitchen**

22. Press F8 to center the text top to bottom.

23. Press Esc to return to the BOTTOM MENU.

24. Print and save the sign-up sheet.

Printing Letterheads as Banners

In the Letterhead project, you can print in sizes up to ten times larger than the regular letterhead size to create banners. These banners, however, print out on individual pages and need to be assembled.

Using Full Panels for Banners

You can print any full panels available in the Letterhead project across an entire banner as illustrated in Figure 3.11.

Create the example in Figure 3.11 following the steps below to see how easy it is to design. Enter the SELECT GRAPHIC LAYOUT menu as you did in the previous example.

1. From the SELECT GRAPHIC LAYOUT menu, select Full Panel.

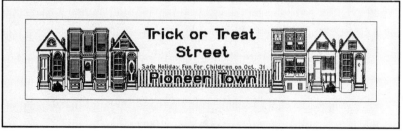

Figure 3.11: In the Letterhead project, you can print a full panel graphic across the entire banner.

2. From the CHOOSE FULL PANEL menu select HOUSES.

3. Highlight Text and press ↵.

4. Choose MADERA font in SOLID style.

5. Type **Trick or Treat** on the first line.

6. Press ↵ for a new line.

7. Press F3, and then choose MADERA font again.

8. Type **Street**.

9. Use the TINY font for the third line and type **Safe Holiday Fun For Children on Oct.31**.

As you can see by the position of the cursor relative to the bottom margin tabs, you will need to change the bottom margin before you can type the next line on the fence.

10. Press F7 to change margins.

11. Highlight Move Bottom Margin, then press ↵.

12. Press ↓ twice to move the cursor, then press ↵ to accept the current cursor position as the new bottom margin.

13. Highlight Done and press ↵.

14. Press ↵ to begin a new line.

15. Press F3, then choose MADERA again.

16. Type **Pioneer Town**.

17. Preview your work.

18. Press any key to continue.

19. Press Esc to return to the TOP MENU.

20. Select Bottom of Letterhead to get to the Print or Save option.

21. Highlight Print or Save and press ↵.

Printing large sizes can overheat your printer. To avoid this, either print a draft-quality copy or reduce the contrast level.

22. Set the print quality to Enhanced Final Quality.

23. Set the contrast level to Light.

24. Select the size of the printout.

Sizes up to six times the normal size will print across the width of one page, but seven times the normal size or more will print across the width of two pages.

Test the paper position. For large-size printouts, the paper position test will place a slash mark on the side and dots on the perforation.

Now you can print and save the banner.

Creating Banners with Graphics in the Middle

In the Letterhead project, you can use any of the graphic layouts available for letterheads in your banners. This means you can place graphics throughout your banner, another feature you cannot accomplish in the Banner project.

One way to get graphics throughout your banner is to start with a row of graphics, and then erase some of them. Let's create the example shown in Figure 3.12 to see how easy it is to design this type of banner. Start by entering the SELECT GRAPHIC LAYOUT menu as in the previous example.

1. From the SELECT GRAPHIC LAYOUT menu, select Small Center Row.

2. Choose GRAPHICS Hi Res and select the BASEBALL graphic.

3. Highlight the 2nd graphic, then press the spacebar to erase it.

4. Erase the 3rd, 4th, 7th, 8th, and 9th graphics the same way.

Figure 3.12: By starting with a row of small graphics and then erasing some of them, you can place graphics throughout your banner.

5. Highlight the last graphic, then press C to change it.

6. Press F2 to select a new graphic by number.

7. Type 34 for the SOCCER graphic and press ↲ twice to select it.

8. Highlight the 3rd graphic from the left, then press C to change it.

9. Press F2, then type 17 and press ↲ twice to select the FOOT-BALL graphic and return to the TOP MENU.

10. Highlight the 2nd graphic from the left, then press C to change it.

11. Press F2, then type 3 and press ↲ twice to select the BASKET-BALL graphic and return to the TOP MENU.

12. Highlight Text and press ↲.

13. Choose AMADOR font in the SOLID style.

You can create this text in one line and still have it fit in the two spaces.

14. Press the spacebar 8 times and type **SPORTS** in capital letters. Then on the same line press the spacebar 13 times and type **SIGN UP**. Press the spacebar 7 more times.

15. Press F8 to center the type top to bottom.

16. Press F10 to preview your work.

17. Press any key to continue.

18. Press Esc to return to the TOP MENU.

19. Choose Bottom of Letterhead, then select Print or Save.

Now you can print the design in a large size to make a banner.

You Can Print and Paint Backdrops for Displays

Scenes such as the VILLAGE letterhead panel can be printed out six times the normal size and used as a backdrop for a diorama or other display. A village backdrop was printed this way and painted with water-colors to use behind a scene of Christmas caroler dolls on a bookshelf.

4 *Making Banners*

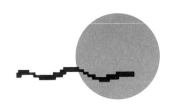

If you need a banner for any occasion—to advertise a sale, promote a workshop, welcome a speaker, or wish someone a happy birthday—The New Print Shop allows you to print banners one or two pages wide, with graphics on the ends, any length you want.

Use the three ready-made banners to give you some ideas and get you started designing your own.

With The New Print Shop you can make horizontal or vertical banners. You can use any of the fonts that come with the program. The text can be placed in one or two lines in four different layouts on the horizontal banners and one line on the vertical banners.

The New Print Shop lets you put large graphics and full panel graphics on either one end or both ends of the banner. You can use more than one graphic and flip the graphics vertically and horizontally.

You may use any of the thin borders to place a trim on the top and bottom of the horizontal banners and down each side of the vertical ones.

In the Banner project an OVERVIEW box takes the place of the PREVIEW box found in the other projects, presenting a diagram rather than a picture of the banner you are creating. You can, however, preview your design while you are creating it. Since the banner is too large to be seen on the screen at one time, you will only be able to view a section at a time. To see how this works, let's preview the three ready-made banners.

Previewing the Three Ready-Made Banners

The Banner project of The New Print Shop program comes with three ready-made banners:

- The Birthday banner is a vertical banner with the cake slice graphic at the top and the ice cream cone graphic on the bottom.

- The Congratulations banner is a horizontal banner that uses the blue ribbon graphic.

- The Go Team banner is a horizontal banner that uses the football graphic.

Let's preview these banners on screen to get acquainted with the project. We'll begin at the MAIN MENU (Figure 4.1).

1. On the MAIN MENU highlight Banner, then press ↵.

2. Highlight Use a Ready Made on the menu, then press ↵.

3. BANNERS is already highlighted. Press ↵ to select it.

The next screen gives you a list of ready-made banners to choose from. Birthday 1 is highlighted.

4. Press ↵ to select Birthday 1.

The BANNER MENU now appears (Figure 4.2). There is a diagram of the banner in the OVERVIEW box. The BANNER MENU lists these options:

Graphics

Message

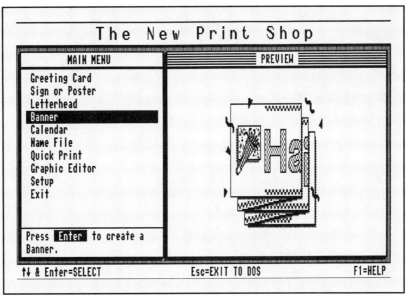

Figure 4.1: To use the Banner project, highlight Banner on the MAIN MENU and press ↵ to select it.

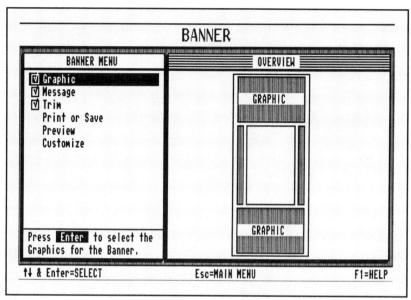

*Figure 4.2: The BANNER MENU lists your options. A diagram of the banner is
displayed in the OVERVIEW box.*

Trim

Print or Save

Preview

Customize

Although the OVERVIEW box presents only a diagram, you can
preview the design at any time. Let's try it.

5. Highlight Preview on the menu, then press ↵.

Only part of the banner is visible at any one time when you preview
it (Figure 4.3). You press ↵ to continue viewing the rest of it.

6. Press ↵ to see the middle of the banner.

7. Press ↵ to see the end of the banner.

8. Press ↵ to return to the BANNER MENU.

9. Press Esc to return to the MAIN MENU.

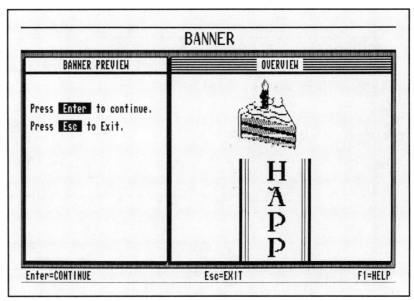

Figure 4.3: Only part of the banner is visible at any one time when you preview it. You press ↵ to continue viewing the rest of it.

A dialog box now warns you that you are about to loose your creation if you haven't saved it. This banner is already saved on the disk.

    10. Press ↵ to select Exit to Main Menu.

Preview the second ready-made banner.

    1. Repeat steps 1 through 3 from the previous example.

    2. Highlight Congratulations, then press ↵.

This is a horizontal banner. The OVERVIEW area shows that it has a graphic at either end and a border on the top and bottom.

    3. Highlight Preview on the BANNER MENU, then press ↵.

    4. Press ↵ several times to view the rest of the banner.

    5. Press Esc to return to the MAIN MENU.

Use the same procedure to view the third ready-made banner.

Designing Your Own Banners

Creating banners is one of the easiest projects in The New Print Shop. Let's create a few to explore the possibilities.

Creating a Horizontal Banner

Begin by creating the horizontal banner illustrated in Figure 4.4. This horizontal banner uses a small line over a large line and a large graphic at each end. The small line is a good way to use a sponsor's name, a person's name, or a date.

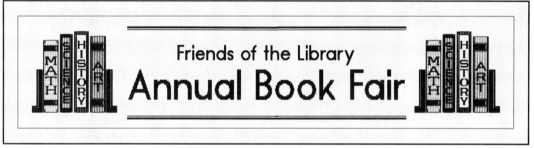

Figure 4.4: This horizontal banner uses a small line over a large line and a large graphic at each end.

1. Highlight Banner on the MAIN MENU.
2. Press ↵ to select it.
3. Highlight Design Your Own, then press ↵.

The TYPE OF BANNER menu now allows you to choose a horizontal or vertical layout for your banner.

4. Horizontal is highlighted on the next menu. Press ↵ to select it.
5. Graphic is highlighted on the next menu. Press ↵ to select it.

The SELECT GRAPHIC LAYOUT menu lists the options that are available for graphic placement (Figure 4.5).

6. Large Graphic Both Ends is highlighted. Press ↵ to select it.

7. GRAPHICS Hi Res is highlighted on the next menu. Press ↵ to select it.

8. Highlight BOOKS, then press ↵.

9. Press ↵ to return to the BANNER MENU.

When you return to the BANNER MENU, Message is highlighted. It's time to put words on this banner.

10. Press ↵ to select Message.

11. From the NUMBER OF LINES menu, highlight Small Line Over Large, then press ↵.

The fonts that are available for the Banner project are the same as those for the other projects in The New Print Shop. AMADOR, the first

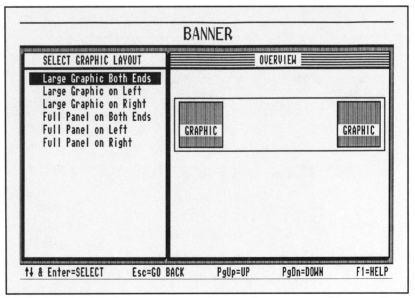

Figure 4.5: The SELECT GRAPHIC LAYOUT menu lists the options that are available for graphic placement.

selection on the current menu, is highlighted. Let's choose it for a big, bold look.

12. Press ↵ to select AMADOR.

13. SOLID is highlighted on the STYLE menu. Press ↵ to select it.

The ENTER TEXT box offers a working area for you to type your text (Figure 4.6). Let's type in the message.

14. On the first line, type **Friends of the Library**.

15. Press ↵ to begin a new line.

16. Type **Annual Book Fair**.

17. Press F10 to preview your banner.

It's a good idea to preview your design while you are still in this working screen. Then you can easily make any changes to the text if you don't like the way it looks.

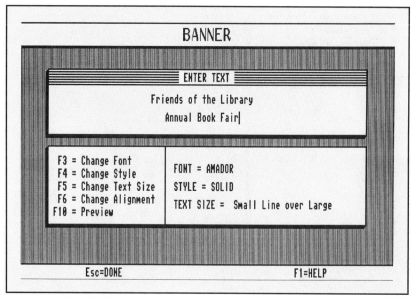

Figure 4.6: The ENTER TEXT box offers a working area for you to type your text.

18. Press ↵ several times to see the whole banner.

19. Press Esc twice to return to the BANNER MENU.

Narrow border trims put a nice finishing touch on the banners. Trim is already highlighted on the BANNER MENU.

20. Press ↵ to select BANNER MENU.

21. Thin <Original> is highlighted. Press ↵ to select it.

22. Highlight DECO. Press ↵ to select it.

Although you previewed your banner when you were typing the message, it's a good idea to give it a final check before printing it.

23. Highlight Preview, then press ↵.

24. Press ↵ several times until you have seen all of your design.

25. Press Esc to return to the BANNER MENU.

Now you can print your banner.

26. Highlight Print or Save, then press ↵.

The PRINT OR SAVE MENU is similar to the ones used in the other projects. Before printing your banner, you will need to change some settings.

Printing long banners can cause overheating in some printers. To avoid this, change the Set Print Quality to Standard Draft Quality or the Set Contrast Level to Light.

27. Highlight Set Print Quality, then press ↵.

You have two choices on this menu—Standard Draft Quality and Enhanced Final Quality. The Standard Draft Quality is the default setting. It prints much faster but also much lighter than the Enhanced Final Quality. For this example, let's set the print quality to Enhanced Final Quality and reduce the contrast level to Light.

28. Highlight Enhanced Final Quality, then press ↵.

29. Highlight Set Contrast Level, then press ↵.

30. Highlight Light, and then press ↵.

Before you print, you should select the size you want for your banner. The default setting is 1-page wide. If you want to print a larger banner, you can highlight SELECT SIZE and choose a 2-page width. For this example, let's print in the 1-page width. Skip this setting this time.
You are ready to print. Print is already highlighted.

31. Press ↵ to select Print.

Your banner should be printing. When you are finished, you can save the design if you want using the same procedure in the Banner project as in the other projects.

How to Use More Than One Graphic in a Banner

You can use more than one graphic in either the horizontal or vertical banners. Let's create the horizontal banner illustrated in Figure 4.7 to learn how to do this. This banner uses two lines of equal size, one graphic at the beginning, and another graphic at the end.

1. Repeat steps 1 through 7 in the last example.

2. Highlight COMPUTER, then press ↵.

3. Press → to highlight the right graphic.

4. Press C to change it.

5. Press Pg Dn once to bring up the menu with PRINTER on it.

6. Highlight PRINTER and press ↵ to select it.

7. Press the F10 key to preview your change.

The graphics will appear side by side because you haven't added any text yet.

8. Press ↵ to continue.

9. Press ↵ to return to the BANNER MENU.

Message is highlighted on the BANNER MENU.

10. Press ⏎ to select Message.

The NUMBER OF LINES menu allows you to choose the number of lines for your message. Let's create the message in two equal lines.

11. Highlight Two Equal Lines, then press ⏎.

When you have a long message, you may want to choose a smaller font to keep the size of the banner small. For this banner, choose a medium-size font, MADERA.

12. Highlight MADERA font and press ⏎ to select it.

13. Choose SOLID from the next menu.

14. Type **Computer Workshop**. Press ⏎ to begin a new line.

15. Type **Demonstration of The New Print Shop**.

Figure 4.7: This banner uses two equal size lines, one graphic at the beginning, and another graphic at the end.

16. Press Esc.

On a single banner, adding trim helps hold the graphic and text together. Let's add a double line to this one. On this menu, Trim is already highlighted.

17. Press ↵ to select Trim.

18. Press ↵ to select THIN <Original>.

19. Highlight Double Line, then press ↵.

20. Highlight Preview and take a look at your creation.

21. Press Esc to return to the BANNER MENU.

22. Highlight Print or Save, then press ↵.

Print your banner using the same procedure as you used in the first example.

Creating a Vertical Banner

Vertical banners can be posted in tall, narrow places such as on support columns or hung from above. The one shown in Figure 4.8 was designed to hang above a display of new products to call attention to the display. Let's create it to discover how vertical banners differ from horizontal ones and to learn how to flip a graphic.

1. Once in the Banner project, select Design Your Own.

2. Highlight Vertical, then press ↵.

3. Graphic is highlighted. Press ↵ to select it.

4. Large Graphic Both Ends is highlighted. Press ↵ to select it.

5. GRAPHICS Hi Res is highlighted. Press ↵ to select it.

6. Press F2 to select a graphic by number.

7. Type 24, the number of the party favor graphic.

8. Press ↵ three times to select the graphic and return to the BANNER MENU.

In Customize flip the bottom graphic so that it faces the other way.

   9. Highlight Customize on the BANNER MENU, then press ↵.

10. Press ↵ to save a temporary copy of your design.

On the screen that appears, only a few commands are available for you to use in the Banner Project (see Figure 4.9).

11. Press ↓ to highlight the bottom graphic.

12. Press the F key on your keyboard to flip the graphic.

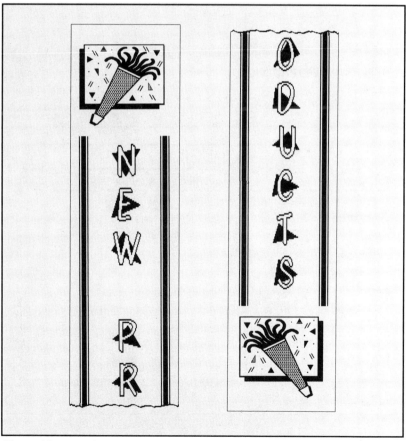

Figure 4.8: Vertical banners can be posted in narrow places or hung in the middle of
a room.

13. Press H to flip the graphic horizontally.

An illustration of the flipped graphic appears on your screen.

14. Press any key to continue.

15. Press Esc to return to the BANNER MENU.

Message is now highlighted on the BANNER MENU. Since you cannot use graphics in the center of the banner, you can use a fancy type such as MARIN to give an illusion of graphics.

16. Press ↵ to select Message.

17. Highlight the MARIN font, then press ↵.

18. SOLID is highlighted. Press ↵ to select it.

19. Type **NEW PRODUCTS**.

20. Press Esc to return to the BANNER MENU.

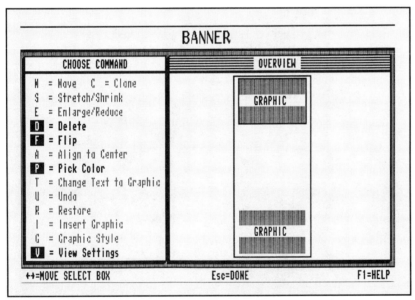

Figure 4.9: In the Banner project, Customize has only a few commands that you can use.

Let's put a thin trim down each side.

21. Trim is highlighted. Press ↵ to select it.
22. THIN <Original> is highlighted. Press ↵ to select it.
23. Highlight Ribbon, then press ↵.
24. Select Preview and look at your design.
25. Press Esc to return to the BANNER MENU.
26. Print your banner.

Exploring Other Options

Using color graphics and unique fonts and trims can create some unusual effects for your banners. And, you can use two or more banners together for additional effects. Let's take a look at some of these options.

Using Color Graphics

The New Print Shop program comes with several color graphics that can be used if you have a color printer. The sale sign on the banner in Figure 4.10 is one of those. The cake shown later in Figure 4.13 is another.

If you don't have a color printer, you can still use these graphics by converting them to black and white. For instructions on converting graphics, see Chapter 10.

The banner in Figure 4.10 is an example of the single-line text layout with a graphic on both ends. It was created with the AMADOR font in SOLID style, and a Ribbon trim was added.

Using Two or More Banners Together

You can acheive additional effects in the Banner project by using two or more banners together.

Figure 4.10: The sale sign is one of the color graphics available in The New Print Shop program.

If you create two or more banners and print them one after another on a single strip of paper, you can place a graphic in the middle of your banner as shown in Figure 4.11.

This banner was created by first making a sign that had a sale graphic in front and no graphic at the end. The same font and trim were used as that in the original sale sign in Figure 4.10.

Note that after printing the first banner, which had no graphic at the end, the printer stopped at the end of the printing. It did not form feed to the end of the page. After printing the second banner, with the graphic at

Figure 4.11: You can place a graphic in the middle of a banner by printing two banners on a single strip of paper.

the end, the printer did form feed to the end of the page. So if you are planning to stack banners end to end, you might want to remember you can place graphics at the beginning of each banner, but on the end of only the last banner if you want the printout to come out right.

You can also create two or more banners to be hung, or stacked. This is similar to the procedure used in the signs for the refreshment stand in Chapter 2.

*U*sing Unusual Fonts

Although you can use graphics only on the ends of banners in the Banner project, you can achieve the effect of graphics by using one of the fancy fonts that are available in The New Print Shop Program or in additional software that is available to use with the program.

The banner in Figure 4.12 was created using the BALLOONS font from the Party Edition of The New Print Shop Graphics Library. For more information on additional software and fonts for use with The New Print Shop, see Appendix C.

The banner in Figure 4.12 is an example of the Large Line over Small text layout. No trim was used.

*U*sing Graphic Trims

You can add extra graphics to your banners by using thin borders made up of tiny graphics. More of these are available in The New Print

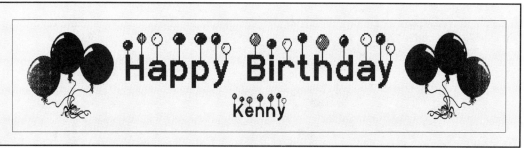

Figure 4.12: *This banner was created using the BALLOONS font from the Party Edition of The New Print Shop Graphics Library. It shows an example of the Large Line over Small text layout.*

Shop Graphics Library. The banner in Figure 4.13 was created using a birthday cake border from the Party Edition.

You can make additional borders of tiny graphics available by converting the original Print Shop borders for use in The New Print Shop. For instructions on converting graphics from Print Shop to use with The New Print Shop Program, see Chapter 10.

Using Special Paper

Special banner paper is available in many office supply stores or computer supply stores. Banner paper is a continuous strip that does not have tear perforations, and often comes on a roll.

By using banner paper you can avoid problems with paper tearing at the perforations. (You can also place a strip of tape along the perforations on the back of your banner to give it more strength.)

Colored paper can add a new dimension to your banners. Colored continuous-feed paper is available in pastel and bright colors. Colored printer ribbons are also available in a variety of colors.

Figure 4.13: Add extra graphics to your banners by using thin borders made up of tiny graphics.

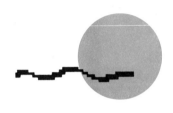

5 *Creating Calendars*

The calendars you can create in The New Print Shop give you the ability to tackle problems requiring organization, such as these:

- You need to do advance planning for your business or organization for the next three years.

- You are publishing a monthly newsletter to coordinate the activities of many committees in your service organization.

- You are in charge of scheduling a weekly car pool.

- You need to straighten out the confusion of who uses a practice room at what time of day.

The Calendar project of The New Print Shop can create yearly, monthly, weekly, and daily calendars for any year from 1901 to 9999.

Each calendar has a top, middle, and bottom. The top and bottom are similar in design to those used in the Letterhead project. All of the graphics and fonts of The New Print Shop are available to use in the top and bottom designs, and the Customize feature allows you to make changes and adjustments. Unlike the Letterhead project, the top and bottom of the Calendar project do not have a default type setting. All lines of type will have the same font and style that you originally selected unless you change the font or style setting.

The middle section varies with the type of calendar you are creating.

- The yearly calendar creates a printout of the months for the year you have chosen. If you have a color printer, you can choose a specific color for this middle section.

- The monthly calendar allows you to enter text and graphics for each day. You can add and revise text and graphics.

- The weekly calendar can begin on any day of the week that you choose. In each daily slot you can add a graphic and up to seven lines of text.

- The daily calendar has hourly slots from 8 a.m. to 6 p.m., in which you can add a graphic and up to four lines of text.

All of the calendars can be saved, reloaded, and revised at any time. They can be printed in the standard 8½-by-11-inch size or in large sizes.

The large sizes are printed in vertical strips just like the vertical signs in the Sign project.

To learn what the Calendar project can do, let's create sample yearly, monthly, weekly, and daily calendars.

Creating a Yearly Calendar for Long-Range Planning

Do you need a calendar for next year, the year after, or for three or six years from now? Let's create a calendar for the year 1996 to be used for planning sales campaigns for a small business. This calendar will look like the one in Figure 5.1.

Selecting the Type of Calendar and Year

The first thing you need to do is select the Calendar project, then choose the type of calendar and the year for the calendar you want to create.

1. Highlight Calendar on the MAIN MENU, then press ↵ to select it.

On the next menu you can choose between designing a new calendar or loading one that you have created before. Design Your Own is already highlighted.

2. Press ↵ to select Design Your Own.

3. When you are asked to select the kind of calendar, highlight Yearly and press ↵ to select it.

You will now be asked to select a year for your calendar. You will need to erase the last two numbers and enter the ones you want.

4. Press Backspace twice to erase the last two numbers.

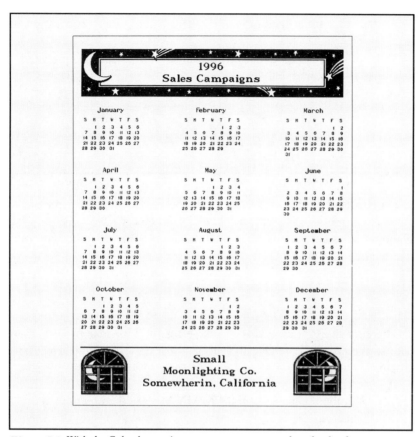

Figure 5.1: With the Calendar project you can create a yearly calendar for any year from 1901 to 9999.

5. Type in **96** as the year for this calendar.

6. Press ⏎ to continue.

Designing the Top of the Yearly Calendar

The first Calendar screen, CALENDAR: Top, now appears (Figure 5.2), and allows you to choose from the following commands to create the top design:

Graphic

Message

Ruled Line

Middle of Calendar

Customize

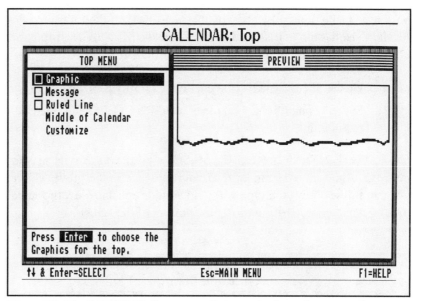

Figure 5.2: The CALENDAR: Top screen allows you to choose the commands to create the top of your calendar.

To create the top and bottom of this calendar, you will use a procedure similar to the one used to create letterheads. Let's begin with Graphic, which is already highlighted on the menu.

7. Press ↵ to select Graphic.

The SELECT GRAPHIC LAYOUT menu now appears to allow you to choose the layout you wish to use for the top of the calendar.

8. Highlight FULL PANEL, then press ↵.

9. On the CHOOSE FULL PANEL menu, highlight MID-NIGHT, then press ↵.

When you return to the CALENDAR: Top screen, Message is high-lighted in the TOP MENU. Let's create the message now.

10. Press ↵ to select Message.

The SELECT FONT and SELECT STYLE menus are the same as the ones used in the other projects. You may select any of the fonts or styles for the Calendar top or bottom designs. Since the MIDNIGHT full panel is narrow, let's choose a medium size font for the message.

11. On the SELECT FONT menu, highlight SIERRA, then press ↵.

12. SOLID is highlighted on the SELECT STYLE menu. Press ↵ to select it.

The ENTER TEXT screen (Figure 5.3) allows you to type in your message. Although you cannot read your message in the preview area, you can still see how your type will fit in your design and view the actual message in the composition box at the bottom of the screen.

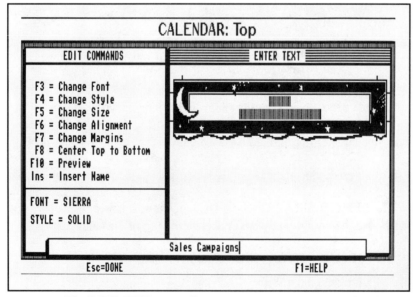

Figure 5.3: The ENTER TEXT screen allows you to type your message and see how your type will fit into your design.

The year 1996, which you selected earlier, is already entered on the top line. Although the year is entered automatically when you begin your message, it would not have appeared on your calendar if you had not chosen to create a message.

13. Press ↵ to begin a new line.

14. Type **Sales Campaigns**.

15. Press F8 to center your design.

16. Press F10 to check your design.

17. Press any key to continue.

18. Press Esc to return to the CALENDAR: Top screen.

Ruled Line is highlighted on the menu now, but you won't need a line with this full panel. Now that you've finished designing the top of the calendar, let's go to the middle section.

19. Highlight Middle of Calendar, then press ↵.

A Look at the Middle of the Calendar

There are only two choices on the menu for the middle of the yearly calendar—Pick Text Color and Bottom Menu (Figure 5.4). If you have a color printer, you could choose Pick Text Color to print the middle in a different color.

Now you'll create the bottom of the calendar.

20. Press ↵ to select Bottom Menu.

Placing a Company Name in the Bottom Space

The CALENDAR: Bottom screen is just the same as the CALENDAR: Top screen except that it includes the Print or Save option instead of Middle of Calendar.

Let's begin by choosing a graphic. Graphic is already highlighted.

21. Press ↵ to select Graphic.

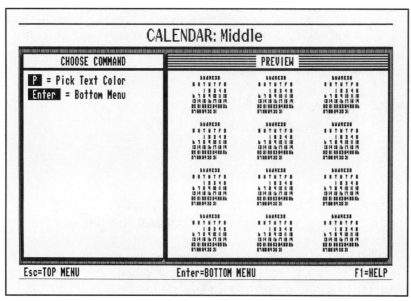

Figure 5.4: There are only two menu choices for the middle of the yearly calendar..

22. Press ↓ eight times to highlight Medium Ends, then press ↵.

23. Press ↵ to select GRAPHICS Hi Res from the next menu.

24. Highlight NIGHT SKY, then press ↵.

25. Press ↵ to return to the CALENDAR: Bottom screen.

Both graphics face the same direction. Let's flip the right graphic to make it face into the page. To do this you will need the Customize feature.

26. Press ↓ three times to highlight Customize, then press ↵.

A dialog box now asks if you want to save a temporary copy of your design.

27. Press ↵ to save a temporary copy of the calendar.

28. Press → once to highlight the right graphic.

29. Press F then H to flip the graphic horizontally.

30. Press Esc to return to the BOTTOM MENU.

Now you can add the company name.

31. Highlight Message, then press ↵.

32. Press ↵ to select SIERRA.

33. Press ↵ to select SOLID.

34. Type **Small.**

35. Press ↵ to begin a new line.

36. Type **Moonlighting Co.**

37. Press ↵ to begin a new line.

38. Type **Somewherin, California.**

39. Press F8 to center the message.

40. Press F10 to check your work.

41. Press any key to continue.

42. Press Esc to return to the BOTTOM MENU.

Ruled Line is highlighted on the BOTTOM MENU when you return to the CALENDAR: Bottom screen. Let's use a thick line to separate the bottom design from the middle.

43. Press ↵ to select Ruled Line.

44. Highlight Thick Line, then press ↵.

How to Print and Save the Yearly Calendar

The procedure for printing and saving the Calendar is the same as that used for the other projects.

45. Press ↵ to select Print or Save from the BOTTOM MENU.

46. Set the print quality to Enhanced Final Quality.

47. Test the paper position.

48. Print this sample calendar in the standard 8½-by-11-inch size.

49. Save your design.

You may want to save your designs on a separate floppy disk. Even if you have a hard disk, you may find that it is easier to organize your collection of creations on floppy disks.

Designing Monthly Calendars for Newsletters

More and more monthly newsletter editors are adding a calendar of events as a regular feature. Large service organizations and many churches have found the monthly calendar an excellent way to remind their members of important dates and times.

For the following example, pretend that you are the newsletter editor of an active social and community service organization. You need to prepare a newsletter like the one in Figure 5.5 for October.

You attend the monthly board meeting of the organization on the first Monday of September to obtain information for your newsletter for the following month. Since you work one month in advance, it is hard to get committee chairmen to get their information to you on time. You offer to put pictures in the calendar for their events if they give you the information at the board meeting. If it comes in later, you just enter the notice with text.

Let's create the newsletter in Figure 5.5.

1. Once in the Calendar project, select Design Your Own.

2. From the TYPE OF CALENDAR menu, highlight Monthly and press ↵.

3. Highlight the month of October and press ↵.

4. Once in the SELECT YEAR menu, change the year to 1995.

5. Press ↵ to continue.

Designing the Top of the Monthly Calendar

On the TOP MENU of the CALENDAR: Top screen, Graphic is highlighted.

Figure 5.5: Many monthly newsletters have a calendar of events like this one.

6. Press ↵ to select Graphic.

7. Highlight Full Panel on the SELECT GRAPHIC LAYOUT menu, then press ↵.

8. Highlight NEWMEX.

9. Press F10 to view the graphic.

10. Press any key to continue.

11. Press ↵ to select this full panel.

Message is now highlighted on the TOP MENU.

12. Press ↵ to select Message.

13. On the SELECT FONT menu, choose SMALL.

14. On the SELECT STYLE menu, choose SOLID.

When the date is entered automatically on the ENTER TEXT screen, it seems to be lost in the design. Do not worry about it now—this problem will be corrected later when you center the text.

15. Press ↵ to begin a new line.

16. Press F3 to change the font on this line.

17. Select SIERRA from the SELECT FONT menu.

18. Type **Dates To Remember.**

19. Center the text by pressing F8.

20. Press F10 to view your work.

Notice that when you center the text while your cursor is still on the second line of type, this second line will be too close to the design. Let's fix this problem.

21. Press any key to exit the preview.

22. Press F8 to remove the centering.

23. Press ↵ to begin a new line, and then press F8 to center the text.

24. Press F10 to view the correction, and then press any key to continue.

25. Press Esc to return to the TOP MENU.

Sometimes just using the cursor like this is the easiest way to position the text.

You do not need a ruled line with this panel design, so go on to the middle of the calendar.

26. Highlight Middle of Calendar on the TOP MENU, then press ↵.

Creating the Middle of the Monthly Calendar

The CALENDAR: Middle screen for the monthly calendar (Figure 5.6) offers many opportunities for creating a complex calendar by allowing you to enter graphics and text for each date.

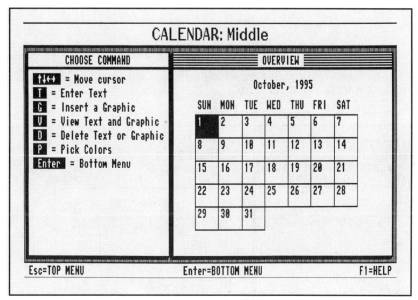

Figure 5.6: *The CALENDAR: Middle screen for the monthly calendar allows you to enter graphics and text for each date.*

27. Press → to highlight the square for Monday, October 2.

28. Press G to insert a graphic.

You must go through the following selection process for each graphic entry you want on the calendar.

29. Press ↵ to select GRAPHICS Hi Res.

30. Highlight IN BOX, then press ↵.

31. With the highlight still on October 2, press T to enter text.

A small composition box appears on the screen to show you the message for a particular day on the calendar as you type it in.

32. Type the following message, pressing ↵ at the end of each line:

     Board

     Meeting

     7 p.m.

33. Press Esc.

You want to make sure that the words don't print over the graphic. View your entry to see how the graphic and text will print together. Figure 5.7 shows the October 2 entry.

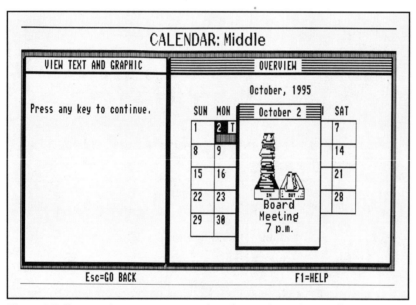

Figure 5.7: You can view your entry to see how the graphic and text will print together.

34. Press V to view your entry for October 2.

35. Press any key to continue.

36. Highlight October 6.

37. To insert the COMPUTER graphic, first choose GRAPHICS Hi Res and then select the graphic.

38. Enter the following text for October 6 as you did for the October 2 entry.

    Computers

    For Schools

    Committee

39. Using Figure 5.6 as a guide, add all the entries that include graphics to your own calendar.

*U*sing the Bottom Space

When you have entered all the information that you received at the board meeting (those entries containing graphics), you can go on to designing the bottom. For this issue, you want to emphasize a big event coming in November.

40. Press ⏎ to go to the BOTTOM MENU.

41. Graphic is highlighted. Press ⏎ to select it.

42. Choose FULL PANEL.

43. Choose LIBRARY from the list of full panel graphics.

44. Message is highlighted on the BOTTOM MENU. Press ⏎ to select it.

45. Press ⏎ to select SIERRA.

46. Press ⏎ to select SOLID.

47. Type the following lines:

    Annual

    Used Book Fair

    November 11

48. Press Esc.

You do not need a ruled line with this panel design.

If you were the newsletter editor for this publication, you would probably save the calendar now and write the rest of the newsletter. Just before publication, you would load it onto your computer and add last minute information. Or you could add information as you received it.

Now, however, go back to the middle and finish creating the rest of the entries. You can go backward through The New Print Shop screens by pressing the Esc key.

49. Press Esc to return to the CALENDAR: Middle screen.

50. Add the text entries without graphics as shown in Figure 5.6.

When you have finished making all the entries, the CALENDAR: Middle screen will look like Figure 5.8.

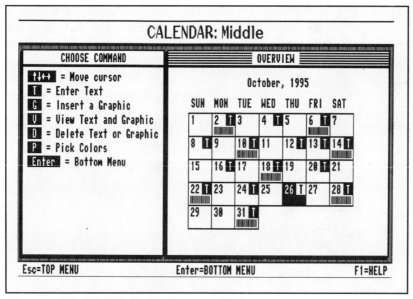

Figure 5.8: The CALENDAR: Middle screen will show many entries when completed.

*P*rinting Your Monthly Calendar

Now you can print and save your monthly calendar. First return to the BOTTOM MENU, then follow the printing instructions that you used in the last example. If you have previously saved an earlier version of this calendar, you can overwrite the old file or you can give the finished calendar a new file name when you save it.

51. Press ⏎ to go to the BOTTOM MENU.

52. Highlight Print or Save, then press ⏎.

53. Highlight Save and overwrite the old file (if you have one).

54. Set the print quality.

55. Test the paper position.

56. Print your monthly calendar.

How to Plan a Weekly Calendar for Carpool Drivers

Weekly calendars can also help organize groups of people by reminding individuals of jobs they are expected to do and when they should do them.

For this example, lets say that you are in charge of organizing transportation for a group of preschoolers. You must schedule parents to pick up and drive five children to and from their preschool. The parents are very cooperative but tend to forget their days unless reminded. Rather than phone each driver every day, you decide to use The New Print Shop to create weekly calendars, such as the one shown in Figure 5.9, for your carpool drivers.

Let's create the weekly calendar in Figure 5.9 to demonstrate how the weekly version differs from the yearly and monthly ones.

1. Once in the Calendar project, select Design Your Own.

2. Choose Weekly from the TYPE OF CALENDAR menu.

3. Choose October from the next menu.

4. Change the year to 1994.

The weekly calendar can begin on any day that you want. The CHOOSE DAY menu allows you to choose the day on which you wish

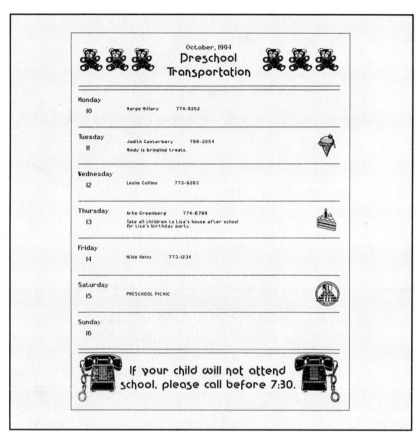

Figure 5.9: A weekly calendar for a preschool carpool reminds parents who is driving on each day.

to start your weekly calendar (Figure 5.10). Since the preschool runs from Monday to Friday, let's begin the weekly calendar on Monday, October 10.

5. Highlight October 10, then press ↵.

Creating a Theme with the Top Graphic

The CALENDAR: Top screen for the weekly calendar is the same as the ones you used for the other calendars, as is the procedure for designing the top section.

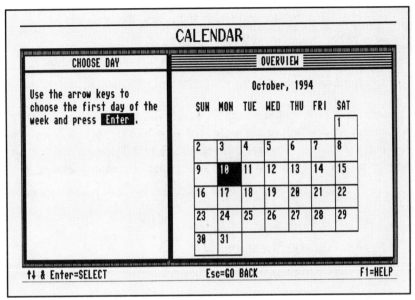

Figure 5.10: The CHOOSE DAY menu allows you to choose the day on which you wish to start your weekly calendar.

Since you are creating a calendar every week, you can add some variety by changing the graphics each time. This also helps the parents use the right calendar. For the week of October 10, you decide to use favorite stuffed animals as the theme of the calendar.

Graphic is already highlighted on the TOP MENU.

6. Press ↵ to select Graphic.

7. Press End to highlight the last choice, Small Staggered II, then press ↵.

8. Press ↵ again to select GRAPHICS Hi Res.

9. Press F2 to select a graphic by number.

10. Type 36 for the teddy bear graphic, then press ↵ twice.

Now you will need to erase the four middle teddy bears to make room for the message. As soon as you have selected the graphic, you have the opportunity to change or erase some of them.

11.   Highlight the 4th teddy bear, then press the spacebar to erase it.

12.   Repeat the last step to erase the 5th, 6th, and 7th teddies.

13.   Press ↵ to return to the CALENDAR: Top screen.

Message is highlighted on the TOP MENU. When you select it you will need to choose a font and style. The month and year will be entered automatically on the first line of the ENTER TEXT screen, and will appear in whatever font and style you select once you enter Message.

14.   Press ↵ to select Message.

15.   Choose SMALL font and SOLID style.

16.   Press ↵ to begin a line below the date.

17.   Press F3 to change the font.

18.   Select SONOMA font.

19.   Type the following lines:

Preschool

Transportation

20.   Press F8 to center the text.

21.   Press F10 to check your work.

22.   Press any key to continue.

23.   Press Esc to return to the CALENDAR: Top screen.

Ruled Line is highlighted on the TOP MENU. Choose a thin rule for the top section.

24.   Press ↵ to select Ruled Line.

25.   Thin Line is highlighted. Press ↵ to select it.

Putting Extra Information on the Bottom

You do not need to create the top, middle, and bottom of your calendars in this order. As in the monthly calendar example, you can create part of the calendar in advance and store it. Then revise your calendar and print it when you need it.

26. Middle of Calendar is now highlighted. Press ↵ to select it.

27. Press ↵ to go to the BOTTOM MENU.

28. Select Graphic from the BOTTOM MENU.

29. From the SELECT GRAPHIC LAYOUT menu, choose Medium Ends.

30. Choose GRAPHICS Hi Res.

31. Select TELEPHONE from the list of graphics.

The bottom space can be used to add some information or remind members of particular rules or regulations.

32. Choose SONOMA font in SOLID style.

33. Type **If your child will not attend** and press ↵ to begin a new line.

34. Type **school, please call before 7:30.**

35. Press F8 to center the text.

36. Press F10 to check the text.

37. Press any key to continue.

38. Press Esc to return to BOTTOM MENU.

39. Select Customize and save a temporary copy of your design when the dialog box appears.

40. Highlight the right graphic and press F and H to flip it horizontally.

41. Press Esc to return to the BOTTOM MENU.

42. Select Ruled Line and choose Thin Line.

How to Use a Blank Calendar for Planning

Now print out a blank copy of your calendar. Save the design you have created on disk to finish later when you have all the carpool information.

43. Save your design using OCT10CP as the file name.

44. Print out a copy of the blank calendar.

You can use the blank calendar to make a rough draft of a schedule. Write in names and phone numbers in pen or pencil. Add notes and special instructions. Then when you have everything ready, load the saved calendar and finish your creation.

Now let's finish the carpool calendar.

45. Once in the Calendar project, choose Load a Saved Calendar.

46. Select OCT10CP and press ↵ to load it.

47. From the TOP MENU, select Middle of Calendar.

Adding Text and Graphics to the Middle

The CALENDAR: Middle screen for the weekly calendar menu appears (Figure 5.11), allowing you to enter text or graphics for each day of the week. Monday is highlighted.

48. Press T to enter text.

A composition box appears and you may now type your message. You can enter up to seven lines of text for each day.

49. Type **Marge Millary**.

50. Press the spacebar ten times and type **774-9202**. Your screen should look like the one in Figure 5.12.

51. Press Esc to return to the CALENDAR: Middle screen.

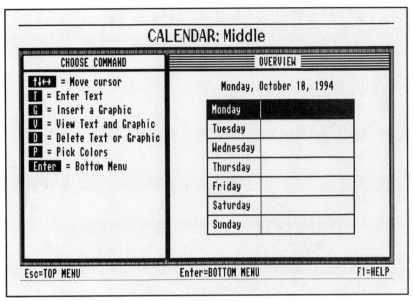

Figure 5.11. The CALENDAR: Middle screen for the weekly calendar allows you to enter text or graphics for each day of the week.

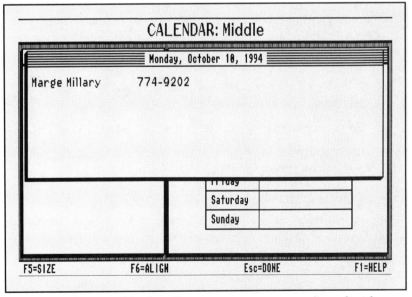

Figure 5.12: The composition box allows you to enter up to seven lines of text for each day.

Let's add a graphic to the Tuesday slot to remind the driver that one of the children is bringing something special. The graphic selection procedure is the same as you have used in other projects.

52. Highlight Tuesday.

53. Press G to enter a graphic.

54. Press ↵ to select GRAPHICS Hi Res.

55. Press F2 to select a graphic by number.

56. Type 18 for the ice cream cone graphic and press ↵ twice to select it.

57. With the highlight still on Tuesday, press T to enter text.

58. Type **Judith Canterbery**, press the spacebar ten times, and type **766-2054**.

59. Press ↵ twice to skip one line.

60. Type **Mindy is bringing treats.**

61. Press Esc.

When you view your text and graphics you will only be able to see part of it on your monitor, just as when you try to view a banner in the Banner project.

62. Press V to view your text and graphic, using → to view each section, then press ↵ to continue.

63. Press ↵ again to return to the CALENDAR: Middle screen.

64. Using the procedures just discussed, add the rest of the text and graphics shown in Figure 5.10 to your calendar.

You are ready to print your calendar—but wait a minute! Leslie Collins has just called to tell you she can't drive on Friday and has traded days with Hilde Heinz. You need to make some changes to the calendar.

65. On the CALENDAR: Middle screen, highlight Wednesday.

66. Press D and then T to delete the text.

67. Press T to enter new text.

68. Type **Leslie Collins**, press the spacebar ten times, then type **773-9283**.

69. Highlight Friday, then press D and then T to delete the text.

70. Enter **Hilde Heinz**, press the spacebar ten times, then type **773-1234**.

71. Press ↵ to return to the BOTTOM MENU, then select Print or Save.

72. Save your design. You will need to overwrite the previously saved file or give this one a new file name.

73. Change the Number of Copies setting to make enough copies for each driver and yourself.

74. Print your weekly calendar.

Getting Organized with a Daily Reservation Calendar

A daily calendar can be created to schedule appointments. The calendar in Figure 5.13 was made to be posted outside a practice room to list the times that individuals had reserved the room. Let's create this calendar to learn how the daily calendar differs from the other kinds of calendars you've already made.

1. Highlight Calendar on the MAIN MENU and press ↵ to select it.

2. Choose Design Your Own.

3. Choose Daily from the TYPE OF CALENDAR menu.

4. Highlight March, then press ↵.

5. Change the year to 1995. Press ↵ to continue.

The next menu allows you to select the date for the daily calendar.

6. Highlight 15, then press ↵ to select it.

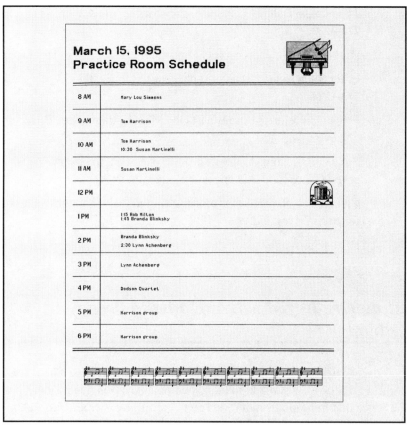

Figure 5.13: A daily calendar such as this one can be created to schedule appointments.

Varying the Top Design

You are now ready to begin creating the top of the daily calendar. Let's use a graphic on the right and align the type on the left.

7. Choose Graphic from the TOP MENU.

8. Select Medium Right from the SELECT GRAPHIC LAYOUT menu.

9. Choose GRAPHICS Hi Res.

10. Press F2 to choose the graphic by number. Type 26, the number for the piano graphic.

11. Press ↵ three times to select the graphic and return to the TOP MENU.

Now add a message to the top. Message is already highlighted.

12. Press ↵ to select Message.

13. Select the MADERA font in the SOLID style.

14. Press F6 to align the date on the left side of the page.

15. Press ↵ to begin a new line.

16. Type **Practice Room Schedule.**

17. Press F8 to vertically center the message.

18. Press F10 to check your work.

19. Press Esc to return to the CALENDAR: Top screen.

20. Select Ruled Line, then choose Thick Line.

21. Highlight Middle of Calendar, then press ↵.

Creating Hour-by-Hour Schedules

The CALENDAR: Middle screen for the daily calendar (Figure 5.14) allows you to enter information in time slots from 8 a.m. to 6 p.m. You can enter a graphic and up to four lines of text in each slot.

The first slot, 8 a.m., is highlighted. Let's enter some text in it.

22. Press T to enter text.

23. Type **Mary Lou Simmons.**

24. Press Esc.

25. Press ↓ to highlight the next time slot, 9 a.m.

26. Press T to enter text.

27. Type **Tom Harrison.**

28. Press Esc.

Not everyone needed to reserve the practice room for a full hour. You will need to split some entries.

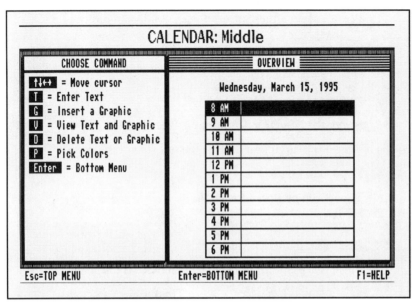

Figure 5.14: The CALENDAR: Middle screen for the daily calendar allows you to enter information in time slots from 8 a.m. to 6 p.m.

29. Highlight the 10 a.m. slot and press T to enter text.

30. Type **Tom Harrison** again and press ↵ twice to leave a blank line before the next line.

31. Type **10:30 Susan Martinelli.**

32. Press Esc.

33. Highlight the 12:00 p.m. slot and press G to insert a graphic.

34. Using the same procedure for adding a graphic as used for the monthly and weekly calendars, select the coffee graphic.

35. Continue entering the rest of the information in the time slots on your calendar.

When you have finished entering text, go to the CALENDAR: Bottom screen to complete your calendar.

36. Press ↵ to go to the BOTTOM MENU.

Sometimes you may only want either a graphic or text in the bottom area. Let's add a row of graphics to the bottom of the calendar.

37. Highlight Graphic and press ↵.

38. Choose the Small Center Row layout.

39. Choose GRAPHICS Hi Res.

40. Select MUSIC. Press ↵ twice to select the graphic and return to the BOTTOM MENU.

There will be no message on the bottom, but you will need a thick ruled line to finish the design.

41. Highlight Ruled Line, then press ↵.

42. Choose Thick Line.

43. Print and save your calendar.

Printing Large Calendars

The Calendar project will print large sizes the same way as the Sign project. You can create a wall-size calendar to coordinate efforts in a classroom, office, or other location.

The large sizes print in vertical strips and must be trimmed and assembled.

Print a sample calendar. Let's take the monthly calendar you created earlier in this chapter and print it one size larger.

1. Load the saved monthly calendar.

2. Move through the menus until you reach the BOTTOM MENU, then select Print or Save.

3. Highlight Select Size.

4. From the CHOOSE SIZE menu, choose 2 times, the next size larger than a single sheet of paper.

5. Print the calendar.

Ideas for Using Calendars

Calendars can be used for long-range planning, coordinating activities, or suggesting activities. You can create calendars with future dates or past dates, then fill them in or leave them blank. The following sections provide a few more suggestions for getting you started in creating your own calendars with The New Print Shop.

Using Yearly Calendars for Organization Planning

Many community and service organizations begin their year in September and end activities in May. It is often hard to get members of these organizations to think about March, April, and May at the first meetings in the fall. By printing out a yearly calendar for this period of time and asking members to highlight with pen or pencil the important dates, it's easier to get everyone thinking in terms of the entire year and how they will schedule major events.

It's often necessary to make business plans for several years in the future, but it's often hard to find calendars that list specific dates for those years. The New Print Shop program will generate a calendar for any year from 1901 to 9999.

Coordinating Group Activities

When several people are trying to work together, a calendar can help tell them who is doing what and when. A large calendar on the wall in a journalism class helps get the newspaper out on time. A calendar in a business lunchroom lists training sessions scheduled. An advent calendar in a church school classroom helps youngsters plan activities leading up to a special event.

Suggesting Activities

Calendars can also suggest activities. For instance, a garden shop owner may create a monthly calendar with tips on things to do at different times of the year. Daily and weekly calendars can remind patients when to take medication and family members when to do chores.

*U*sing Blank Calendars

Blank calendars can be used as sign-up sheets when people are needed to volunteer their time. They can also be used to keep daily and weekly records of things done, money spent, and so on.

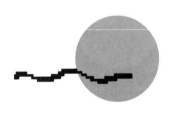

6 *Using the Name File*

Let's say you have just finished a training workshop and need to make 15 certificates for the participants that completed the classes. Your task would be much simpler if you could make a list of all the names and somehow have those names automatically printed on the certificates.

Fortunately, the Name File feature in The New Print Shop program allows you to do just that. It puts those names automatically into the cards, certificates, and awards that you create.

In the Name File you create a list of names, adding, deleting, or editing names on this list as you wish. You can save the list or print it out. But most importantly, you can merge the list with your other projects to produce multiple, personalized copies of your projects.

You can select names from the list and print only those names. And you have the choice of printing either full names or just first names.

If one name is too long to fit into your certificate, a dialog box will appear on screen to let you know. You can then skip that name and adjust it later.

Let's create a name file to see how it works. In the following example you will make a list of participants in a computer training workshop and make certificates of achievement for them using the certificate you created in Chapter 2.

Creating a Name File

You enter Name File the same way you enter the five main projects in The New Print Shop.

1. Highlight Name File on the MAIN MENU and press ↵ to select it.

The NAME FILE screen (Figure 6.1) allows you to add, delete, edit, or select names on your list. It also allows you to print or save the list.

Deleting Old Names

When the NAME FILE screen appears, there are some names already on it. Let's start by deleting one or two of them.

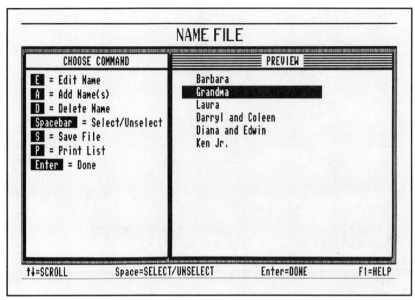

Figure 6.1: The NAME FILE screen allows you to add, delete, edit, or select names on your list. It also allows you to print or save the list.

2. Highlight one of the names on the list.

3. Press D to delete the name.

A dialog box will appear and ask you to confirm that you really do want to delete this name.

4. Press ↵ to delete the name.

5. Using the same procedure, delete another name.

*A*dding New Names

Now add the names of the workshop participants.

6. Press A to add names to the list.

The screen changes (Figure 6.2) to allow you to type in the names.

7. Type in **Tim Kelly**.

8. Press ↵ to enter it into the list.

9. Using the same procedure, add the following names:

   Charles Hill

   Ann Moore

   Allen Schlenkowitz

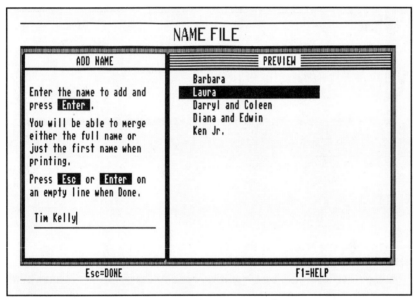

Figure 6.2: After you press A you can add names to your list.

*E*diting Existing Names

There is an error in the spelling of one of the names. You will need to edit it.

10. Highlight **Ann Moore**.

11. Press E to edit the name.

12. In the edit box, backspace to erase the last name and add an **e** to the end of **Ann**, then retype **Moore**.

13. Press ↵ to enter the name onto the list.

*P*rinting Out a Copy of the Name File

Let's print out a copy of the list for you to keep as a record of who will receive the certificates. Be sure your printer is turned on. When you hit P, your printer will begin printing immediately.

14. Press P to print a copy of the list.

*S*electing Names to Be Used

Now let's select the names that you want to use on the certificates. When you press the spacebar while a name is highlighted, a check mark is placed in front of the name you have chosen (Figure 6.3).

15. Highlight **Tim Kelly**, then press the spacebar to select the name.

16. Highlight **Charles Hill** and press the spacebar.

17. Using the same procedure, select **Anne Moore**, and then **Allen Schlenkowitz**.

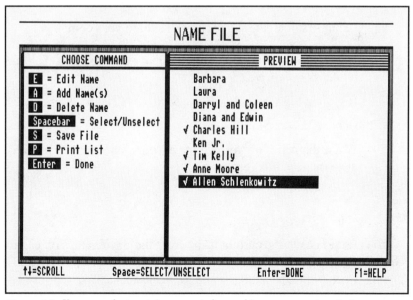

Figure 6.3: You can select certain names to be used in your current project.

Save the file so that you can use it later.

18. Press S to save the file.

You will be told by a dialog box that the file has been saved. You have finished creating the name file and can now return to the MAIN MENU.

19. Press any key to continue.

20. Press ↵ to return to the MAIN MENU.

Using the Name File to Print Certificates

To learn how to use the Name File you have just created, let's take the certificate that you made in Chapter 2 for the Computer Training Workshop and print out additional certificates with the names you have selected.

Loading a Saved Sign

You need to first load the saved certificate onto your computer.

1. If you saved the certificate on a separate disk, insert that disk into your disk drive.

2. Highlight Sign or Poster on the MAIN MENU, then press ↵.

3. Choose Load a Saved Sign.

4. When the menu of saved signs appears, choose the file name that you gave this certificate.

Deleting the Name from the Certificate

You need to delete the current name from the certificate. You cannot choose Message to delete the name because you converted the text to a graphic when you adjusted the name to fit the space. You will need to use the Customize feature.

5. Highlight Customize.

6. Skip the saving process by selecting Enter Customize without saving.

7. Highlight **Allen Schlenkowitz**.

8. Press D to delete the name.

9. Press Esc to return to the SIGN MENU.

Now let's tell The New Print Shop to look for the Name File, where to print the name, and what font to use to print it.

10. Highlight Message, then press ↵.

11. Choose the MERCED font from the SELECT FONT MENU.

12. Choose SOLID from the SELECT STYLE menu.

13. Press ↓ twice to place the cursor on the line where the name used to be.

14. Press the Insert key (Ins) on your keyboard.

<NAME> will be inserted in this space. This tells the program to use the Name File. When you press the F10 key to view your work or after you press Esc to return to the SIGN MENU, the certificate should look like the one in Figure 6.4.

*P*rinting the Certificates with the Name File

Now let's print out the certificates using the draft-quality setting to produce them more quickly.

15. Press Esc to return to the SIGN MENU.

16. Highlight Print or Save on the MAIN MENU and press ↵ to select it.

17. Select Print.

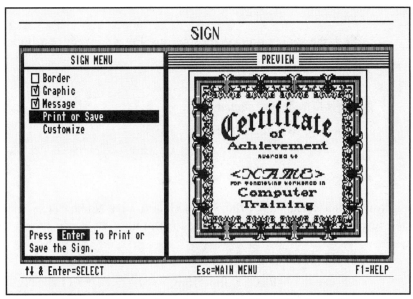

Figure 6.4: When you press the Insert key to use the Name File, the certificate on your screen will look like this.

18. When a dialog box appears to ask if you want to select names, choose No, use the ones already selected.

If you had not selected names or want to change the selected names, you could do so now. When no names are selected, a dialog box asks you to select names or cancel.

Another dialog box appears with the following choices:

Merge First name only

Merge Full names

Cancel

19. Choose Merge Full name.

20. Print the certificates.

The certificates that the Name File creates will look like the one shown in Figure 6.5.

When the merge function gets to the name **Allen Schlenkowitz**, a dialog box will appear telling you that this name will not fit. You will have the opportunity to skip it. Since this entry was included only to show what happens when a name is too long, you can skip it.

Figure 6.5: The Name File will create certificates like this for each of the names you selected.

Ideas for Using the Name File

The Name File can be used for any names or lists, not just for names of people. Whenever you need multiple, customized copies, consider using the Name File to help you get the job done.

Creating Thank-You Cards for Sponsors

A list of names could consist of classes in a show or exhibit, and cards can be made to thank sponsors of the different classes. A list of the classes could be compiled in the Name File and the thank-you card created in the Greeting Card project. The name of a class would then be inserted in each greeting card (Figure 6.6) and a card printed for each sponsor.

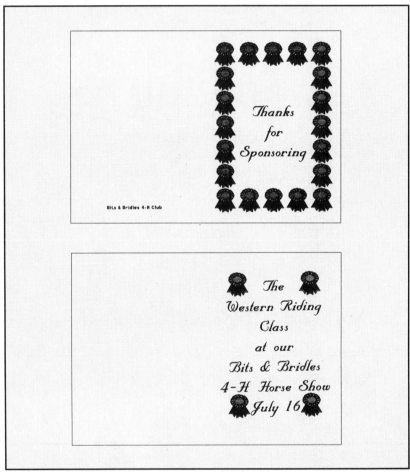

Figure 6.6: This card thanks a sponsor who contributed money to buy the ribbons and trophies for one class of a 4-H horse show. The outside of the card is shown at the top, and the inside shown below.

*O*rganizing a Book Sale or Store with Category Signs

Whenever you need to arrange things in categories, create signs to identify the various categories. The sign in Figure 6.7 could be used to identify the mystery books on a table at a book fair or shelves in a used bookstore.

The sign in Figure 6.7 was created in the Sign project with the book border from the School & Business Edition of The New Print Shop Graphic Library and the book graphic and SUTTER font from The New Print Shop. A Name File of book categories included the category **Mystery**.

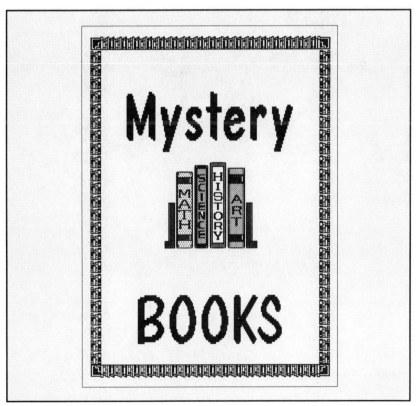

Figure 6.7: This sign could be used to identify the mystery books on a table at a book fair or shelves in a used bookstore.

Using Only Letters or Numbers

A registration table may divide registrants according to the letters of their last name. Signs for these tables—A-E, F-I, etc.—can be created in the Sign project and printed with a Name File (Figure 6.8).

Figure 6.8: To separate registrants according to the letters of their last name, create signs like this with a Name File list and the Sign project.

Signs to identify different exhibits can be created from a name file that uses only numbers (Figure 6.9).

Figure 6.9: A name file that contains only numbers can be used to make signs such as this one.

7 *Using Quick Print*

There may be times when all you want to print out is a single picture or a few words. For instance:

- You need a line of large type to paste in a newsletter because your word processor can't create large letters.

- You need a few phrases and a couple of graphics for a bulletin board display you are creating.

The Quick Print feature of The New Print Shop provides the help you need in these situations.

Quick Print can print out a single line of type or a single graphic.

You can use any of the fonts that come with the program to print a line the width of a single page. The number of characters in this line will vary with the size of type you choose.

You can print any of the graphics that come with the program in a small, medium, or large size. If you have a color printer, you can print in color.

Your printer will form feed after printing. If you choose to print only one copy, you will have one line of type or one graphic on a page. If you choose two or more copies, you will print them on the same page. Quick Print will not print out different graphics or lines of text on the same page.

Let's create a text and a graphic example to see how this works.

Quick Print a Line of Text

Whenever you need a single line of text you can use Quick Print. Begin by highlighting Quick Print on the MAIN MENU (Figure 7.1).

1. Highlight Quick Print on the MAIN MENU and press ↵ to select it.

You can now choose between text and graphics. We'll start with text.

2. Highlight Text, then press ↵.

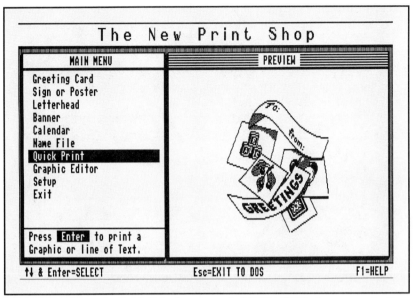

Figure 7.1: Choose the Quick Print feature on the MAIN MENU when you need a line of type or a single graphic.

The same SELECT FONT and SELECT STYLE menus that you have been using in the other projects will appear next.

   3. Highlight the AMADOR font, then press ↵.

   4. Highlight the OUTLINE style, then press ↵.

An ENTER TEXT box on the QUICK PRINT screen (Figure 7.2) now allows you to type your one-line message. The number of characters that can fit on this line will depend on the size font you are using.

   5. Type **This is a sample line of text**.

   6. Press ↵ to proceed to the PRINT MENU.

The PRINT MENU in Quick Print (Figure 7.3), although similar to the print menus that you have used in the other projects, has fewer choices.

   7. Highlight Set Number of Copies on the PRINT MENU, then press ↵.

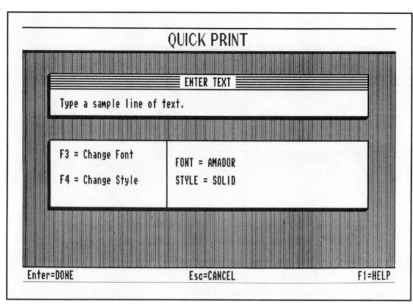

Figure 7.2: An ENTER TEXT box allows you to type one line of text.

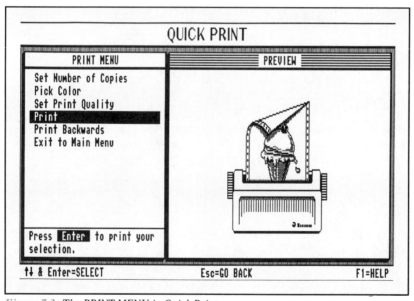

Figure 7.3: The PRINT MENU in Quick Print

8. Type 3 for three copies.

9. Highlight Set Print Quality, then press ↵.

10. Select Enhanced Final Quality.

11. Highlight Print, then press ↵.

Quick Print a Graphic

When you need a single graphic, highlight Quick Print on the MAIN MENU. You will then use the same graphics selection process that you have used in the other projects. Let's print out a copy of the baseball graphic.

1. Highlight Quick Print on the MAIN MENU and press ↵ to select it.

2. When you are asked to choose text or graphics, select Graphics.

3. From the SELECT SIZE menu, select Medium Graphic.

4. Highlight GRAPHICS Hi Res, then press ↵.

5. Select BASEBALL.

6. Print the graphic using the same procedure you followed to print the sample line of text.

8 *Using the Graphic Editor*

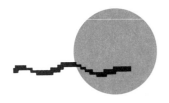

Sometimes the graphics in The New Print Shop aren't quite right for the design you are creating. Perhaps you want to horizontally flip a graphic but can't, because it has words on it. Maybe you want to use only the crayons from the graphic PLAYTIME. Or, you might want to create a line of music that looks like a real line of music with the clefs only at the beginning and no spaces between the measures. With the Graphic Editor you can do all these things and more.

The Graphic Editor is a simple drawing feature that allows you to modify graphics or create new ones of your own.

You can load any Print Shop graphic into the Graphic Editor and perform the following changes on it:

- Draw or erase a line

- Turn individual dots on or off

- Move the graphic

- Flip the graphic horizontally or vertically

- Insert or remove a column or a row

- Create a negative image of the graphic

- Print the graphic

- Save the graphic for later use

Although The New Print Shop uses three sizes of graphics, you work with the small size in the Graphic Editor. When your design calls for a larger size, the program scales then the image for you.

When you modify a graphic in the Graphic Editor, you change a copy of it and create a new graphic. You always have the original version that you can continue to use.

To see how the Graphic Editor works, let's modify three graphics from The New Print Shop, IN BOX, PLAYTIME, and MUSIC, and then create a simple new graphic of your own.

D*eleting Letters on a Graphic*

Sometimes you may want to flip a graphic horizontally. If that graphic includes words, they will be printed backwards when the graphic is flipped.

With the Graphic Editor you can erase the words, then save this new wordless graphic in a special file to use later.

Let's take out the words **IN** and **OUT** from the graphic IN BOX.

1. Highlight Graphic Editor on the MAIN MENU and press ↵ to select it.

The GRAPHIC EDITOR screen (Figure 8.1) now appears. It allows you to choose commands from the menu on the left and preview your work in the box on the right. Below the PREVIEW box is an important message area that you will use often in the following examples. This message area displays the coordinates of the cursor position on the

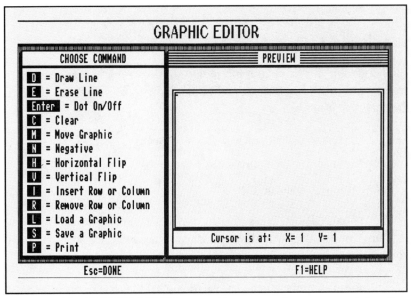

Figure 8.1: The GRAPHIC EDITOR screen allows you to choose commands from the menu on the left and preview your work on the right.

screen. The X number is the horizontal location and the Y number is the vertical location.

In the following examples you may be asked to place the cursor at a particular position, such as (X=10, Y=17). Use the arrow keys to position the cursor. You can press an arrow key once to move the cursor one space, or you can hold the arrow key down to move the cursor continuously. (On some computers you may need to use the shift key with the arrow key to move the cursor quickly.)

Loading the Graphic

Loading a graphic into the Graphic Editor is similar to placing a graphic in one of the projects.

2. Press L to load a graphic.

3. GRAPHICS Hi Res is highlighted on the next menu. Press ↵ to select it.

4. Highlight IN BOX, then press ↵.

Erasing the Words

The graphic IN BOX graphic is now in the preview area. You will erase the words **IN** and **OUT** from the side of the boxes. Begin by placing the cursor near the words.

5. Press ↓ until the cursor reaches (Y = 48).

6. Press → until the cursor reaches (X = 22).

7. Press E to erase a line.

The DRAW OR ERASE menu appears in the box on the left with instructions to use the arrow keys to draw a line and then press ↵ when you are done.

8. Press → eight times to erase the top of the word.

9. Press ↓ once to position the cursor on the next line (Y=49).

10. Press ← eight times to erase more of the word.

11. Press ↓ once to position the cursor on the next line (Y=50).

12. Press → eight times to finish erasing the word.

13. Press ↵ to return to the CHOOSE COMMAND menu.

When you are using the erase command, you will continue to erase wherever you move the cursor. If you tried to move to the second box to erase the word **OUT** with the erase command still on, you would erase everything you passed, and there would be a blank line across the boxes.

Now you are ready to remove the second word.

14. Press the right arrow until the cursor is in front of the word **OUT** (X=60, Y=50).

15. Press E to erase.

16. Press → eleven times (X=71).

17. Press ↑ once to place the cursor on the next line (Y=49).

18. Press ← ten times.

19. Press ↑ once to place the cursor on the next line (Y=48).

20. Press ← eleven times to erase the top of the words.

21. Press ↵ to return to the CHOOSE COMMAND menu.

The words are gone. The new graphic looks like the one in Figure 8.2. You can save this graphic and use it when you need to flip it.

Saving the Graphic to a New File

When you save your graphics, you will first make a file for your own creations. Then you will create a name for the individual graphic and place it in this file. You may want to save your own designs on a separate floppy disk so that they will be easy to locate.

22. Press S to save the graphic.

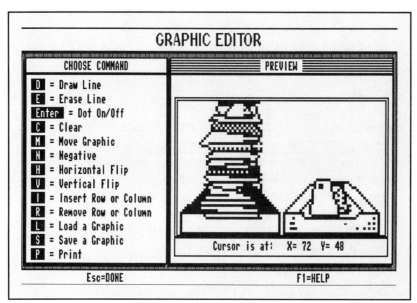

Figure 8.2: *The new graphic looks like this after you have erased the words on the boxes.*

A dialog box now gives you the following choices:

>   Save graphic to a new file
>
>   Save graphic to an existing file
>
>   Cancel

You will need to create a new file.

23.   Press ↵ to select Save graphic to a new file.

24.   Name this new file MYGRAPH, then press ↵ to enter the new file name.

The GRAPHIC NAME box appears to allow you to type in a name for your graphic. The name of the graphic you loaded is listed in the box. Let's add a word to it.

25.   Leave the words IN BOX in the GRAPHIC NAME box and type in **blank** at the end.

26. Press ⏎ to return to the CHOOSE COMMAND menu.

*P*rinting the Graphic

If you want to see what your graphic looks like, you can print out a copy.

27. Press P to print a copy of the graphic.

The printer will start immediately because there is no print menu. The printed graphic will be small and the only one on a page. The printer will form feed when the printing is over.

*C*learing the Screen

Now you need to clear the screen to get ready to work on the next example.

28. Press C to clear the screen.

As soon as you press C, a dialog box will ask if you are sure you want to clear the screen. This is a safety feature in case you accidentally hit the wrong key.

29. Yes is highlighted. Press ⏎ to select it.

*M*odifying a Graphic

Sometimes you may need only a part of a graphic to work into your design. For example, you may need only the crayons from the graphic PLAYTIME or the pencil from the graphic PENS.

Or, you may need a reversed or flipped image. Perhaps you need a slightly larger or slimmer image or want to move the images within the graphic closer together or farther apart.

Let's load the graphic PLAYTIME and learn how the Graphic Editor lets you make these changes.

Selecting a Graphic by Number

1. Press L to load a graphic.

2. GRAPHICS Hi Res is highlighted. Press ↵ to select it.

If you changed drives to save the last graphic, you may need to change back to the previous drive to get the GRAPHICS Hi Res file. Press F9 to change drives.

3. Press F2 to select by number.

4. Type 28 for the graphic PLAYTIME and press ↵ to select it.

PLAYTIME is now highlighted on the SELECT GRAPHIC menu and the picture is illustrated in the GRAPHIC box.

5. Press ↵ to return to the GRAPHIC EDITOR screen.

PLAYTIME is now in the preview area of the Graphic Editor (Figure 8.3).

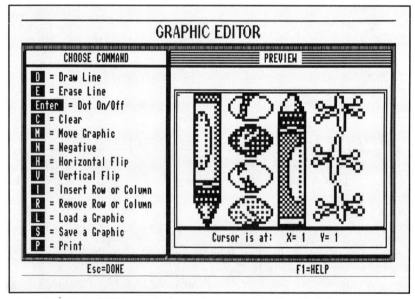

Figure 8.3: PLAYTIME is now in the preview area of the Graphic Editor.

*E*rasing Part of a Graphic

Let's remove the marbles first.

6. Press → until the cursor is at the top of the first marble (X=28, Y=1).

7. Press E to erase the marbles.

8. Press → 13 times (X=41, Y=1).

9. Press ↓ and hold it down until the cursor is at the bottom of the graphic (X=41, Y=52).

10. Press ← 18 times.

11. Press ↑ and hold it down until the cursor is at the top of the graphic (Y=2).

12. Press → 17 times.

13. Press ↓ and hold it down until the cursor is near the bottom of the screen (Y=51).

14. Press ← 16 times.

15. Press ↑ and hold it down until the cursor is at the top of the screen again.

16. Continue erasing until you have removed all of the marbles.

17. Press ↵ to return to the CHOOSE COMMAND menu.

When the marbles have been erased, the graphic will resemble Figure 8.4.

Now let's remove the jacks.

18. Place the cursor at the top of the row of jacks (X=68,Y=1).

19. Press E to erase the jacks.

20. Press → 12 times (X=80, Y=1).

21. Press ↓ and hold it down until the cursor reaches the bottom of the graphic.

22. Press ← once.

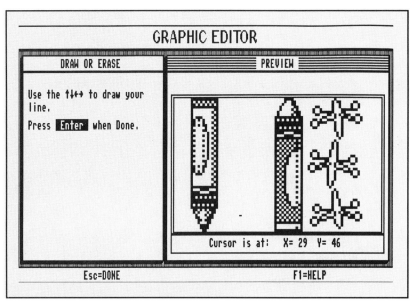

Figure 8.4: When the marbles have been erased, the graphic will look like this.

23. Press ↑ and hold it down until the cursor reaches the top of the screen.

24. Press ← once.

25. Repeat the last four steps until you have erased all the jacks.

26. Press ↵ to return to the CHOOSE COMMAND menu.

When you have finished erasing the jacks, the modified graphic will resemble the one in Figure 8.5.

Centering the Image

The crayons are not centered. In the Graphic Editor you can move the graphic within the screen, but be careful not to move it off the screen. If you do so, it will be erased and you will have to reload the graphic and start over.

Since there is no centering function, you will have to do a little math to calculate the center.

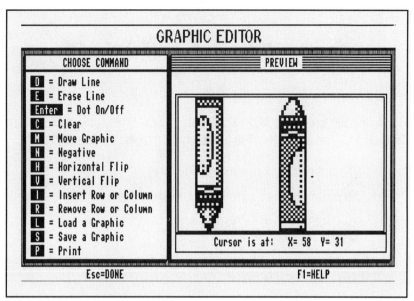

Figure 8.5:When you have finished erasing the marbles and jacks, the modified graphic will have only crayons.

27. Place the cursor on the right side of the graphic as far as it will go (X=88).

28. Press ← until the cursor reaches the edge of the right crayon (X=55).

29. Place the cursor on the left edge of the left crayon (X=8).

You have just measured the distance from the right crayon to the edge. If you subtract the number at the edge of the crayon from the number at the edge of the graphic, you will find that there are 33 spaces on the right (88−55=33). And there are 8 spaces on the left for a total of 41 spaces on both sides. To place the crayons near the middle, you will need 20 spaces on one side and 21 on the other. Since you have 8 spaces on the left, you can move the crayons 12 spaces to the right.

The Graphic Editor moves the whole graphic. You will need to count the number of moves yourself, since the message area won't show cursor position for this movement.

30. Press M to move the crayons.

31. Press → 12 times.

32. Press ↵ to return to the CHOOSE COMMAND menu.

Saving the Graphic to an Existing File

Saving the graphic will be a different process this time, because you have already created a file. Save this graphic to the existing file.

33. Press S to save the graphic.

34. Highlight Save to an existing file, then press ↵.

35. Highlight MYGRAPH, then press ↵. (Change drives if you need to.)

36. In the GRAPHIC NAME box backspace to erase PLAYTIME and type in **CRAYONS**.

37. Press ↵ to return to the CHOOSE COMMAND menu.

Creating a Negative Image of Your Graphic

Sometimes you may want to vary your design with a negative image of a graphic. Let's create one for the CRAYONS and store it in your MYGRAPH file.

38. Press N to create a negative image.

39. Repeat steps 33 through 35 to save the negative image.

40. In the GRAPHIC NAME box type in **Neg** at the end of the line, then press ↵ .

How to Flip Your Graphic

Although you can flip a graphic in Customize, there are times when you will need to flip a graphic before working on it. Let's learn how to do this.

41. Press N to get a positive image once more.

42. Press H for a horizontal flip.

43. If you want to save this graphic, repeat steps 33 to 35 and give it a new name. You could call it CRAYONS HF.

44. Press V for a vertical flip.

45. If you want to save this graphic, repeat steps 33 to 35 and give it a new name. You could call it CRAYONS VF.

46. Press H and V once more to restore the graphic to its original position.

Inserting a Column or Row to Change Your Graphic

Sometimes you may want to make a graphic a little wider or narrower, taller or shorter. You can do this by inserting or deleting a column or row. A row adds or deletes a horizontal line and a column adds or deletes a vertical line. Let's see how this works.

47. Place the cursor on the top row in the middle of the left crayon (X=25, Y=1).

48. Press I, then C to insert a column.

49. Repeat the last step three more times to add a total of four columns.

50. Place the cursor on the top of the right crayon (X=65, Y=1).

51. Press I, then C to insert a column.

52. Repeat the last step three more times to add a total of four columns.

You now have fatter crayons like those shown in Figure 8.6, but you still need to fill in the design. Let's try two ways to do that. Your cursor should still be at the tip of the right crayon (X=65, Y=1).

53. Press D to draw a line.

54. Press → four times to fill in the tip of the right crayon.

55. Press ↵ to return to the CHOOSE COMMAND menu.

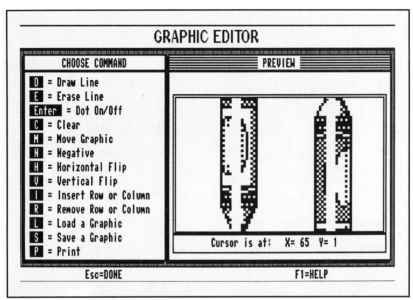

Figure 8.6: *After adding columns to the crayon images, you will need to fill in the design.*

56. Place the cursor at the base of the left crayon (X=25, Y=1).

57. Press D to draw a line.

58. Press → four times to fill in the base of the left crayon.

59. Press ↵ to return to the CHOOSE COMMAND menu.

Drawing a short line is often easier to do dot by dot. Pressing ↵ will add or erase a dot at the current cursor position in the graphic. Let's fill in part of the pattern this way.

60. Position the cursor at (X=26, Y=2).

61. Press ↵ to add a dot there.

62. Add dots at (X=28, Y=2), (X=27, Y=3), and (X=25, Y=3).

Use either method to fill in the crayon design to resemble Figure 8.7. Remember, if you make a mistake and add a dot in the wrong place, just press ↵ again to erase it.

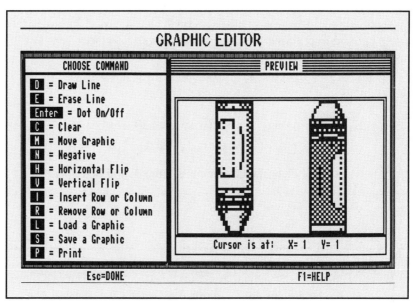

Figure 8.7: *When you have adjusted the pattern, each crayon will be four columns wider.*

Removing Columns to Move Images Within Graphics

When you add a column within a graphic, a column at the right is deleted to make room for this new addition. When you add a row, a row is removed from the bottom of the graphic.

If you want these crayons centered again, you could use the method described earlier. Or, you could simply delete columns elsewhere to move the crayons closer together.

By inserting and deleting rows and columns, you can move an image within the graphic. Let's see how this is done.

63. Place the cursor between the two crayons.

64. Press R, then C to remove a column.

65. Repeat the last step 13 more times to remove a total of 14 spaces between the crayons.

You could remove additional spaces on the left to create a graphic that could be used in the Small Frame graphic layout as shown later in Figure 8.11.

Let's save your graphic now. You can always reload it and do additional things to it later.

66. Save your graphic as you did in steps 33 to 35.

67. Press C to clear the screen.

68. Select Yes, clear the Graphic when the dialog box appears.

Adjusting the Graphic MUSIC for a Line of Music

If you wanted a continuous line of music across the bottom of a letterhead or a calendar, you might be tempted to use the Small Tiled graphic layout for this purpose. This would leave a space between bars and a clef sign in each measure—not exactly the continuous staff you had in mind. (Usually, a line of music will have the clef signs in the first measure only.)

In the Graphic Editor you can modify the graphic MUSIC to create two new graphics, one for the first measure and the other for the following measures. Let's begin with the first measure. You will need to extend the right side of the staff to the edge of the graphic.

Loading the Graphic

Once again the loading procedure consists of a simple graphic selection process.

1. Press L to load a graphic.

2. GRAPHICS Hi Res is highlighted. Press ↵ to select it.

3. Press F2 to select the graphic by number.

4. Type 22 and press ↵ twice to select MUSIC and load it into the Graphic Editor.

*E*xtending Lines

To extend the lines of the staff to the edge of the graphic, you will need to erase the bar at the end of the measure and redraw it.

5. Place the cursor at the right side of the graphic above the bar (X=86, Y=9).

6. Press E, then ↓ to erase the bar.

7. Press ↵ to stop erasing.

8. Press → twice to place the cursor in the last column (X=88, Y=45).

9. Press D to draw a line.

10. Move the cursor to (Y=10).

11. Press ← twice.

12. Press ↵ to stop drawing.

13. Place the cursor at (X=86, Y=13) and press ↵ to add a dot.

14. Press → once and press ↵ to add another dot.

15. Place the cursor on the next line of the staff and add dots to extend this line, too. Extend all the lines this way.

When you need a very short line, it is easier to use the dot-by-dot method than the D key. When you have extended the lines, the graphic will look like the one shown in Figure 8.8.

Save this graphic in your MYGRAPH file before you continue to modify it.

16. Press S to save.

17. Select Save to an existing file, and then choose MYGRAPH.

18. Name this graphic FIRST MUSIC.

*E*rasing the Treble and Bass Clefs

Now erase the treble and bass clefs to create the second graphic.

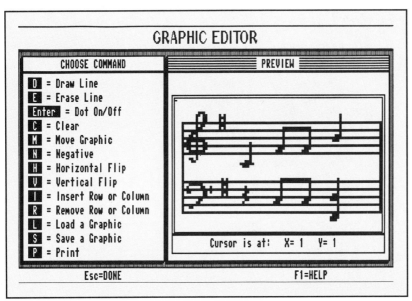

Figure 8.8: Extend the right side of the graphic MUSIC to use it at the beginning of a line of music in a tiled layout.

19. Place the cursor on the upper-left corner of the staff (X=4, Y=9).

20. Press E to erase.

21. Press ↓ and hold it down until the cursor reaches the bottom line (X=4, Y=45).

22. Press → once.

23. Press ↑ and hold it down until the cursor reaches the top of the staff.

24. Continue erasing until you have removed the treble and bass clef signs and the sharp signs as shown in Figure 8.9.

25. Press ↵ to stop erasing.

You will now need to redraw the staff lines to the left edge of the graphic. The instructions below use the D key, but you may use the dot method if you prefer.

26. Place the cursor at (X=23, Y=10).

27. Press D to draw a line.

28. Press ← to move the cursor to the edge (X=1).

29. Press ↓ to move the cursor to (Y=45).

30. Press → to complete the last line.

31. Press ↵ to stop drawing.

32. Place the cursor on the next line of the staff.

33. Press D to draw a line.

34. Press ← to move the cursor to (X=1).

35. Press ↵ to stop drawing.

36. Repeat the last four steps until all the lines are redrawn.

*A*dding New Notes

The lines on the left need a note to balance the design. Let's put a new note in the treble staff and another in the bass staff.

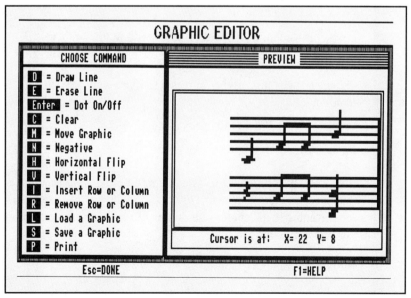

Figure 8.9: To create a graphic that represents a middle measure in a line of music, you must first erase the clef and sharp signs.

37. Place the cursor at (X=20, Y=15).

38. Press D to draw.

39. Press ↑ eight times until the cursor reaches (Y=7).

40. Press ↵ to stop drawing.

41. Place the cursor at (X=19, Y=15). Press ↵ to add a dot.

42. Press ← once, and then press ↵ to add a dot.

43. Press → once and ↓ twice to move the cursor to (X=19, Y=17). Press ↵ to add a dot.

44. Press ← once, and then press ↵ to add a dot.

45. Press ← again, and then press ↵ to add a dot.

Now place a note in the bass staff.

46. Place the cursor at (X=20, Y=32).

47. Press D to draw.

48. Press ↓ seven times to move the cursor to (X=20, Y=39).

49. Press ↵ to stop drawing.

50. Press ↑ once and ← once. Press ↵ to add a dot.

51. Press ← once. Press ↵ to add a dot.

52. Press → once and ↓ twice to move to (X=19, Y=40). Press ↵ to add a dot.

53. Press ← once. Press ↵ to add a dot.

54. Press ← again. Press ↵ to add a dot.

You now have a graphic that represents a middle measure in a line of music (Figure 8.10). If you wanted, you could change a few notes and create a third graphic to alternate with this one to add variety in the note pattern. For now, save this graphic.

55. Press S to save the graphic.

56. When the dialog box appears, choose Save to an existing file.

57. Highlight MYGRAPH and press ↵.

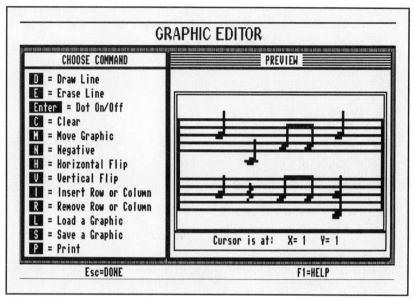

Figure 8.10:This music graphic now represents a middle measure in a line of music.

58. Name this graphic MUSIC 2, then press ↵.

59. Press C, then ↵ to clear the screen.

Creating Your Own Graphics

Sometimes a very simple graphic made with the Graphic Editor, such as an empty box or frame, can be very useful in creating designs.

To draw your own graphics, you can use the same drawing methods you learned to modify graphics.

1. Place the cursor at (Y=1, X=1).

2. Press D to draw.

3. Press → to move to (X=88).

4. Press ↓ to move to the bottom (Y=52).

5. Press ← to move to (X=1).

6. Press ↑ to move to (Y=2).

7. Press → to move to (X=87).

8. Press ↓ to move to (Y=51).

9. Press ← to move to (X=2).

10. Press ↑ to move to (Y=3).

11. Press ↵ to stop drawing.

You have drawn a square border to be used anywhere on the page in any of the projects in The New Print Shop. You could also create other border designs. For now, let's save this graphic. We'll use it shortly.

12. Press S to save the graphic.

13. Select Save to an existing file when the dialog box appears.

14. Highlight MYGRAPH and press ↵.

15. Name this graphic EMPTY BOX. Press ↵ to return to the CHOOSE COMMAND menu.

Using the New Graphics

The graphics you modify or draw in the Graphic Editor are usually created with a purpose in mind—you need a graphic for a particular design. Let's look at some of the products that could use the graphics we modified in the examples above.

Using the Crayon Graphic

Three new crayon graphics are used in a flyer (Figure 8.11) to advertise an afterschool art class for elementary school children. Centered, thin crayons were used in the top and bottom of the Small Frame layout, negative crayon graphics were used in the corners, and adjusted crayon graphics were used on the sides.

The flyer was designed in the Sign project. The crayon border was created by using the Small Frame graphic layout, and the negative corners where entered with the change feature immediately after selecting

Figure 8.11: Three new crayon graphics are used in the Small Frame graphic layout in this flyer.

the graphic. In Customize the right negative graphics were flipped horizontally and every other crayon graphic on the sides was flipped vertically. The graphics on the right side were also flipped horizontally.

The SONOMA font was used in the RAISED and SOLID styles. The SMALL font was used for the grades. In Customize, text was enlarged or reduced and moved.

Creating the Line of Music

The old and the new music graphics are used in the letterhead shown in Figure 8.12. The original graphic MUSIC, which comes with The New

Print Shop, is used in the top. The two new modifications are used to print a line of music across the bottom.

In the top of the letterhead, the MERCED font was used for the name, the SMALL font for the title, and the TINY font for the address. In Customize, the name was enlarged and both the graphic and type moved closer to the center.

To create the line of music for the bottom, the Small Center Row graphic layout and the graphic MUSIC 2 were chosen. Using the change feature, the first graphic MUSIC was replaced by the graphic FIRST MUSIC.

Figure 8.12: Three music graphics are used in this letterhead. The original music graphic appears in the top and the two new modifications create a line of music across the bottom.

Placing a Border Around a Graphic

With the graphic EMPTY BOX you can place a border around graphics in the center of your design, not just around the outside edge of a sign or card. There are several ways to do this. Let's use the Insert Graphic feature in Customize to put a graphic within a graphic (Figure 8.13).

1. Highlight Sign or Poster on the MAIN MENU, then press ↵.

2. Choose Design Your Own.

3. Choose Tall from the next menu.

4. From the SIGN MENU choose Graphic.

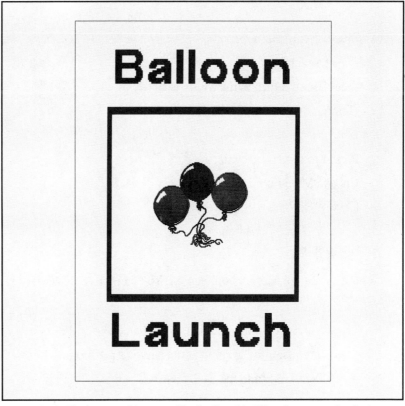

Figure 8.13: The box graphic created in the Graphic Editor becomes a border in this sign.

5. Highlight Large Centered, then press ↵.

6. Instead of GRAPHICS Hi Res, highlight MYGRAPH and press ↵.

7. Highlight EMPTY BOX, then press ↵.

8. Press ↵ to return to the SIGN MENU.

9. Highlight Message, then press ↵.

10. Choose the MADERA font in the SOLID style.

11. Press F5 for large type.

12. Type **Balloon** above the box.

13. Press ↓ several times to move the cursor to the line below the graphic.

14. Press F5 for large type.

15. Type **Launch**.

16. Press Esc to return to the SIGN MENU.

17. Highlight Customize, then press ↵.

18. Enter Customize without saving the design.

19. Press I to insert a graphic.

20. Choose Medium Graphic.

21. Choose GRAPHICS Hi Res this time.

22. BALLOONS is highlighted on the menu. Press ↵ to select this graphic.

A square cursor appears on your screen. You can move this cursor to the location you wish to place the graphic.

23. Press ↓ and → to move the cursor to the center of the page.

24. Press ↵ to insert the graphic at the cursor's position.

25. Press Esc to return to the SIGN MENU.

26. Print and save your flyer.

The graphic BALLOONS now appears inside the graphic EMPTY BOX.

Getting the Most Out of the Customize Feature

The Customize feature in The New Print Shop opens the door to creativity by allowing you to make changes and adjustments in your design. It enables you to take the standard fonts, graphics, and layouts that come with the program and customize them for your own use. For instance:

- The fonts in The New Print Shop can be printed in two sizes—small and large. But in Customize you can enlarge or reduce those sizes.

- The graphics come in three sizes—small, medium, and large. But in Customize you can stretch or shrink them to any size.

- Many graphic layouts are offered for each of the projects. But in Customize you can place graphics anywhere on the page.

Customize cannot be entered from the MAIN MENU. It appears on some of the menus of each of the five projects—Greeting Card, Sign or Poster, Letterhead, Banner, and Calendar. And, you must create something before you can use it, or a dialog box will tell you that there is nothing to customize.

Once you do enter Customize, there is an interesting assortment of choices available on the menu:

Move

Clone

Stretch/Shrink

Enlarge/Reduce

Delete

Flip

Align to Center

Pick Color

Change Text to Graphic

Undo

Restore

Insert Graphic

Graphic Style

View Settings

*E*xploring the Customize Commands

If you have been following the examples in previous chapters, you are already familiar with many of the commands on the Customize menu. But you have only scratched the surface when it comes to the many things that the Customize feature can do for your designs. Let's create the sample flyer shown in Figure 9.1 to explore and review many of the commands in Customize.

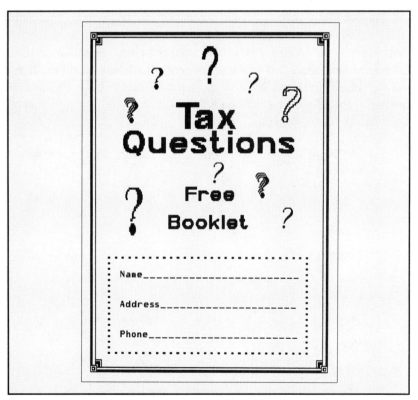

Figure 9.1: Several of the commands in Customize were used to create this flyer.

Plan Before You Begin

Before you begin to create a product in one of the projects in The New Print Shop, you should take a few moments to plan what you are going to do. You should have an idea of what the finished product will look like. You may have already chosen the graphic or know what message you are going to use.

Sometimes this planning will change the order of the things you do to create your design. In the following example, you will need to create some question marks and modify them before you continue with your design.

Creating the Coupon Box

You will need a box graphic for the coupon. You could create one in the Graphic Editor or you can use the empty box you created in the last chapter. The dotted line which is used around the coupon can be created the same way as the empty box. Instead of drawing a solid line, place a dot every three spaces. If you want to make the box with dotted lines, use the following instructions. If you want to use the box you have already created, skip the following instructions and begin at the section on creating the question marks.

1. Highlight Graphic Editor on the MAIN MENU, then press ↵ to select it.

2. The cursor will be in the starting position (X=1, Y=1) when the Graphic Editor screen appears. Press ↵ to add a dot in this location.

3. Press → three times, then press ↵ to add a dot in this location.

4. Repeat step 3 across the top to the right side of the screen (X=88).

5. Press ↓ three times, then press ↵ to add a dot in this location.

6. Repeat step 5 down the right side.

7. Press ← three times, then press ↵ to add a dot in this location.

8. Repeat step 7 across the bottom to the left edge.

9. Press ↑ three times, then press ↵ to add a dot in this location.

10. Repeat step 9 until you reach the top again.

11. Store the graphic in the MYGRAPH file you created in the last chapter. Call the graphic DOTTED BOX.

Creating the Question Marks

The flyer in Figure 9.1 will be created in the Sign or Poster project.

1. Select Sign or Poster from the MAIN MENU.

2. Design Your Own is highlighted. Press ↵ to select it.

3. Tall is highlighted. Press ↵ to select it.

4. Border is highlighted on the SIGN MENU. Press ↵ to select it.

5. Thin is highlighted on the SELECT BORDER FROM menu. Press ↵ to select it.

6. Highlight DECO, then press ↵.

Let's begin with Message to create the question marks.

7. Highlight Message on the SIGN MENU, then press ↵.

8. The AMADOR font is highlighted. Press ↵ to select it.

9. The SOLID style is highlighted. Press ↵ to select it.

10. Type one question mark.

11. Press ↵ to begin a new line.

12. Press F3 to change fonts.

13. Highlight MERCED. Press ↵ to select it.

14. Type one question mark.

15. Press ↵ to begin a new line.

16. Press F3 to change fonts.

17. Highlight VENTURA. Press ↵ to select it.

18. Type one question mark.

19. Press Esc to return to the SIGN MENU.

Customizing the Question Marks

You now have three lines of type with a question mark on each line. Each question mark is in a different font. Let's enter Customize to move those question marks and make room for the message.

20. Highlight Customize, then press ↵.

Before you enter Customize, you will get a dialog box on your screen asking if you would like to save a temporary copy of your design. Normally you do, but now you don't have much to save.

21. Highlight Enter Customize without saving, then press ↵.

On the customize screen (Figure 9.2) the commands are listed on a menu on the left and the preview area is on the right. The dark items on the menu are available to use with text. To get a wider choice of commands, you must convert the text to a graphic.

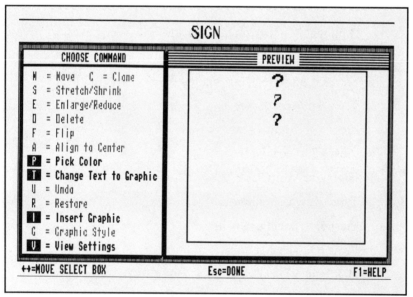

Figure 9.2: On the customize screen the commands are listed on a menu on the left and the preview area is on the right. The dark items on the menu are available for use with text.

22. Press ↓ to move the cursor to the first question mark.

23. Press T to convert the text to a graphic.

A dialog box now warns you that you will no longer be able to edit your text if you convert it. You can, however, always create a new message later.

24. Choose Convert the Text to Graphic.

Figure 9.3 shows the commands that are available to use with graphics. Now that you have changed the text to a graphic these commands are also available to use with lines of type.

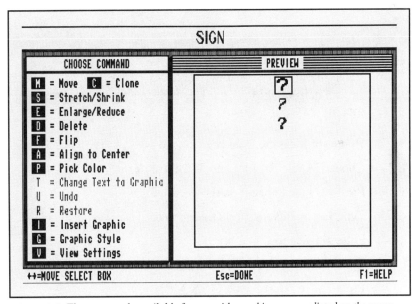

Figure 9.3: The commands available for use with graphics are now listed on the menu.

Now let's move those question marks around to make room for the message you are going to create. The question mark on the first line is highlighted with a blinking cursor around it.

25. Press ↓ to highlight the question mark on the second line.

26. Press M to move this question mark.

The menu on the left side of the screen now changes to give you instructions for moving.

27. Press → nine times, then press ↵ to return to the CHOOSE COMMAND menu.

28. Press ↓ to highlight the question mark on the third line.

29. Press M to move the question mark.

30. Press ← nine times and ↑ twice, then press ↵ to return to the CHOOSE COMMAND menu.

31. Press Esc to return to the SIGN MENU.

Creating the Message

Now create the message for this flyer. Notice that there is no check mark in the box in front of Message. This is because you converted your text to a graphic.

32. Highlight Message, then press ↵.

33. Choose MADERA font and SOLID style.

34. Press ↵ twice to begin on the third line.

35. Type **Tax** on this line and **Questions** on the next line.

36. Press ↵ twice to skip a line.

37. Type **Free** on this line and **Booklet** on the next line.

38. Press Esc to return to the SIGN MENU.

Enlarging and Reducing Type

Now let's use Customize to make some of these words larger and some smaller. You will want to save your work this time.

39. Highlight Customize, then press ↵.

40. When the dialog box appears, save a temporary copy of your design.

41. Press ↓ four times to highlight **Tax**.

42. Press T to change this new text to a graphic and press ↵ to convert the text when the dialog box appears.

43. Press E to enlarge this word.

You now have instructions in the menu box that tell you how to either reduce or enlarge the converted text.

44. Press the + key on your numeric keypad three times to enlarge the cursor, then press ↵ to enlarge the word to fit the cursor.

45. With the cursor still on **Tax**, press A and H to align the word horizontally on the page.

46. Press ↓ to highlight **Questions**.

47. Press E to enlarge this word.

48. Press + two times, then press ↵.

49. Press A and H to align the word horizontally on the page.

50. Highlight **Free**.

51. Press E to reduce this word.

52. Press the − key on your numeric keypad once to reduce the cursor, then press ↵ to reduce the word to fit the cursor.

53. Press A and H to align this word horizontally on the page.

54. Press ↓ to highlight **Booklet**.

55. Press E to reduce this word.

56. Press − once, then press ↵.

57. Press A and H to align this word horizontally on the page.

Inserting the Coupon Graphic

Now it's time to use the box with dotted lines (or the empty box graphic) to create a coupon.

58. Press I to insert a graphic.

59. Highlight Medium Graphic, then press ↵.

60. Highlight MYGRAPH, then press ↵.

61. Select DOTTED BOX (or EMPTY BOX).

A blinking cursor appears in the upper-left corner of your screen. Use it to place the graphic where you want it. The graphic will not be the right size, and you will need to stretch it later.

62. Press ↓ 15 times and → 2 times.

63. Press ↵ to insert the graphic at the cursor's location.

64. Press ↓ to move the blinking cursor to the graphic you just inserted.

65. Press S to stretch the graphic.

66. Press → 12 times to stretch the cursor across the page, then press ↵ to stretch the graphic to fit the cursor.

Cloning the Question Marks

Now clone the question marks.

67. Press ↑ to highlight the left question mark.

68. Press C to clone the question mark.

69. Press ↓ six times to move the cursor to the place you want the clone.

70. Press ↵ to insert the clone in the new cursor position.

71. The highlight is still on the original question mark. Press C to clone it again.

72. Press ↑ twice and → three times to move the cursor.

73. Press ↵ to insert the clone in the new cursor position.

Changing the Graphic Style

Let's change the style of the converted text to vary the appearance of the question marks.

74. Press G to change the style of the highlighted question mark.
75. Highlight 3-D, then press ↵.

Clone some of these 3-D question marks.

76. Press C to clone the question mark.
77. Press ↓ 5 times and → 15 times to move the cursor.
78. Press ↵ to insert the clone at the new cursor position.
79. Press ↑ to highlight the upper-right question mark.
80. Press C to clone this question mark.
81. Press ↓ eight times to move the cursor.
82. Press ↵ to insert the clone at the new cursor position.
83. Press C to clone this question mark again.
84. Press ↑ once and ← three times to move the cursor.
85. Press ↵ to insert the clone at the new cursor position.
86. Press G to change the graphic style again.
87. Choose Outline.

Stretching and Shrinking Graphics

Now let's make some of these question marks bigger and some smaller.

88. Press S to stretch the same question mark.
89. Press → once and ↓ once to stretch the cursor.

90. Press ↵ to stretch the question mark to fit the cursor.

91. Press ← to highlight the top question mark.

92. Press S to stretch the question mark.

93. Press ↓ once.

94. Press ↵ to stretch the question mark to fit the cursor.

95. Press ← until the question mark to the left of **Free** is highlighted.

96. Press S to stretch the question mark.

97. Press ↓ twice and → once to stretch the cursor.

98. Press ↵ to stretch the question mark to fit the cursor.

99. Press → three times to highlight the lower-right question mark.

100. Press C to clone the question mark.

101. Press ↑ three times and ← eight times to move the cursor.

102. Press ↵ to clone the question mark at the new cursor position.

103. Press S to shrink the question mark.

104. Press ↑ once to shrink the cursor.

105. Press ↵ to shrink the question mark to fit the cursor.

That's much too small! You must correct this mistake.

106. Press U for Undo.

See how easy it is to erase your mistakes. And see how easy it is to place graphics all over the page.

Picking Colors for the Question Marks

If you have a color printer, you can choose a separate color for each of these question marks. Even if you don't have a color printer, let's look at the color options.

107. Press P to pick colors.

The menu gives you these choices:

> This Graphic
>
> All Graphics
>
> Behind Everything

108. This Graphic is highlighted. Press ↵ to select it.

Several color choices now appear on the menu.

> Black
>
> Red
>
> Blue
>
> Purple
>
> Yellow
>
> Orange
>
> Green

You can choose any one of these colors and select different colors for different question marks. You can also print the message in different colors.

Adding Type to the Coupon Graphic

Let's go back to the SIGN MENU and finish this flyer.

109. Press Esc three times to return to the SIGN MENU.

110. Highlight Message on the SIGN MENU, then press ↵.

111. Choose the TINY font in the SOLID style.

112. Press ↓ 15 times to move the cursor inside the coupon box.

113. Press F6 to align type on the left.

114. Press the spacebar five times, type **Name**, and press shift and the underline key to create a line across the box.

115. Press ↵ twice to begin a new line.

116. Press the spacebar five times, type **Address**, and use the underline key to place a line across the box.

117. Press ↵ twice to begin a new line.

118. Press the spacebar five times, type the word **Phone**, and use the underline key to place a line across the box.

119. Press F10 to check your work.

120. Press any key to continue.

121. Press Esc to return to the SIGN MENU.

122. Print or save the flyer.

Getting More Out of the Customize Feature

The more you use the Customize feature, the more you will appreciate the flexibility it allows when you create your designs. The best way to get the most out of the Customize feature is to use it often.

Plan to Use Customize

Include the Customize feature in the planning of your projects. Where do you get ideas to use in your planning? You will find many in this book. And you will find many in the mail that comes to your house every day. Take another look at that "junk mail" before you throw it in the trash. Most of it has been created by professional advertising designers, and you should peruse these mailers to get ideas for things you'd like to try with The New Print Shop.

Use Customize for Problem Solving

When you created the certificate in Chapter 2, the program told you the name you wanted to use was too long. You relied on Customize to change the size of the type. When you run into problems trying to create a design, try using Customize to solve them.

When you work with full panels, you will often experience problems that Customize can solve. You may have trouble including the size type you want, the number of words you need, or the placement of the message.

Let's work on a sample full panel poster for a parenting class (Figure 9.4) to learn more about adjusting type sizes and moving type.

1. Highlight Sign or Poster on the MAIN MENU, then press ↵.

2. Design Your Own is highlighted. Press ↵ to select it.

3. Tall is highlighted. Press ↵ to select it.

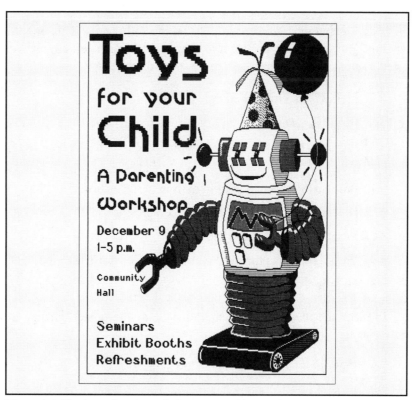

Figure 9.4: You can solve size and placement problems in Full Panel designs by using Customize.

4. Highlight Graphic on the SIGN MENU, then press ↵.

5. Highlight FULL PANEL, then press ↵.

6. Highlight ROBOT (but don't press ↵).

7. Press the F10 key to preview the robot graphic. Then press any key to continue.

8. Press ↵ to select the robot graphic.

9. Message is highlighted on the SIGN MENU. Press ↵ to select it.

10. Choose the SONOMA font in the SOLID style.

*M*oving *Margins*

Often the margins are set too tight on the full panels. This one, for example, only allows space for a message in the upper-left corner. You need to move the margins to use more space on the panel.

11. Press F7 to move the margins.

12. Highlight Move Bottom Margin, then press ↵.

13. Press ↓ 11 times to move the blinking cursor to the bottom of the panel.

14. Press ↵ to move the bottom margin to the cursor's position.

15. Highlight Move Right Margin, then press ↵.

16. Press → twice to move the cursor.

17. Press ↵ to move the right margin to the cursor's position.

18. Highlight Done, then press ↵.

To place the message down the left side of the poster, change the alignment.

19. Press F6 to align type on the left side.

20. Press F5 for large type.

21. Type **Toys**.

22. Press ↵ to begin a new line.

23. Type **for your**.

24. Press ↵ to begin a new line.

25. Press F5 for large type on this line, then type **Child**.

26. Press ↵ to begin a new line.

27. On the next two lines type these words:

> **A Parenting**
>
> **Workshop**

28. Press ↵ to begin a new line.

29. Press F3 to change fonts.

30. Choose the SMALL font.

31. On the next two lines, type the following:

> **December 9**
>
> **1-5 p.m.**

32. Press F3 to change font again and choose TINY.

33. Press ↵ to skip a line.

34. On the next two lines type these words:

> **Community**
>
> **Hall**

35. Press ↵ to begin a new line.

36. Press F3 to change fonts and choose SMALL.

37. Press ↵ to skip a line.

38. On the next three lines type these words:

> **Seminars**
>
> **Exhibit Booths**
>
> **Refreshments**

39. Press Esc to return to the SIGN MENU.

When you finish entering the lines of type, many of the words will be running into the design of the panel (Figure 9.5).

Adjusting the Size of Type to Fit the Panel Design

In Customize you can adjust the size of the type and move the lines of type to fit around a design in the full panels.

40. Highlight Customize on the SIGN MENU, then press ↵.

41. Press ↵ to save a temporary copy of your design.

When you enter Customize, the full panel itself is highlighted and the menu lists the commands that are now available. Note that one of the commands is Flip. Although we will not use it in this example, it is possible to flip the entire panel and have the Robot on the left facing right. You might want to do that another time.

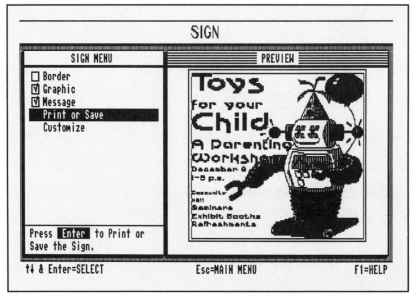

Figure 9.5: When you finish entering the lines of type, many of the words will be running into the design of the panel.

42. Press ↓ once to highlight **Toys**.

43. Press T, then ↵ when the dialog box appears to convert the text to a graphic.

44. Press E to enlarge this line.

45. Press + on your numeric keypad twice, then press ↵ to finish enlarging this line.

46. Highlight the next line.

47. Press M to move this line.

48. Press → once to move the cursor, then press ↵ to move the line to this new cursor position.

49. Highlight **Child**.

50. Press E to reduce this word.

51. Press − on your numeric keypad once, then press ↵ to finish reducing the word.

52. With this line still highlighted, press M to move it. Press → once to move the cursor, then press ↵ to move the line to the new cursor position.

53. Reduce **Parenting** and **Workshop** by pressing E and the − key twice each time. While each line is highlighted, move it one space to the right using the same procedure as in steps 47 and 48.

54. Shrink the next two lines by pressing S, ← once, then ↵ to finish shrinking.

55. Move these same two lines one space to the right by pressing M, → once, then ↵.

56. Move each of the following five lines one space to the right by pressing M, → once, then ↵.

    Community

    Hall

    Seminars

Exhibit Booths

Refreshments

Your poster should now resemble the one in Figure 9.4.

*U*sing Customize to Refine Size and Position

Just as you changed the size and placement of type in the last two samples, you can change the size and placement of the picture graphics.

Create the letterhead in Figure 9.6 to explore some of the refinements possible for the pictures you use.

Figure 9.6: You can change the size and placement of picture graphics in Customize to give greater variety to your designs.

Creating the Top Letterhead Design

Let's begin by creating the graphics and text that you will change in Customize.

1. Highlight Letterhead on the MAIN MENU, then press ↵.

2. Design Your Own is highlighted. Press ↵ to select it.

3. Graphic is highlighted on the TOP MENU. Press ↵ to select it.

4. Select Small Staggered from the SELECT GRAPHIC LAYOUT menu.

5. GRAPHICS Hi Res is highlighted. Press ↵ to select it.

6. Highlight DAISIES, then press ↵.

7. A blinking cursor box highlights the first graphic. Press the spacebar to erase this graphic.

8. Press → to highlight the second graphic, then press the spacebar to erase it.

9. Repeat step 7 for the third graphic.

10. Press ↵ to return to the TOP MENU.

11. Text is highlighted on the menu. Press ↵ to select it.

12. Select VENTURA font in the SOLID style.

13. Press F6 to align text on the left.

14. Type **Tina Pettle** on this line.

15. Press ↵ to begin a new line.

16. Press F3 to change the font from the default font and choose SMALL.

17. Type **Floral Arranging** on this line.

18. Press ↵ to begin a new line.

19. Type **7667 Rose Avenue, Anytown, Kansas 66666**.

20. Press ↵ to begin a new line.

21. Type **Phone 333-4444** on this line.

22. Press F8 to center the type top to bottom.

23. Press F10 to check your work, and then press any key to continue.

24. Press Esc to return to the TOP MENU.

Add the Ruled Line before entering Customize so that you can incorporate it into the new changes of your design.

25. Highlight Ruled Line, then press ↵.

26. Thin Line is highlighted. Press ↵ to select it.

Refining the Top Graphics in Customize

In Customize you will make the left graphic smaller and the right graphic bigger to create a graduated design. Since the enlarging feature uses the right arrow key, you will need to move the last graphic to the left before you can enlarge it.

27. Highlight Customize, then press ↵.

28. Save a temporary copy of your design.

The highlight is on the ruled line when you enter Customize.

29. Press → three times to move the highlight to the last graphic.

30. Press M to move the graphic.

31. Press ← three times to move the cursor, then press ↵ to move the graphic to the new cursor position.

32. With the highlight still on this graphic, enlarge it by pressing E, + four times, then ↵.

33. Press A, then V to align this graphic vertically.

34. Press ← twice to highlight the right graphic.

35. Press E, – twice, then ↵ to reduce the graphic.

36. With the highlight still on this graphic, press M, → four times, then ↵ to move the graphic.

37. Press A, then V to align this graphic vertically.

38. With the highlight on the right graphic, press F, then H to flip it horizontally.

39. Repeat the last step with each of the other graphics.

Refining Text in the Letterhead

Let's use some of the new things you have learned about changing text to adjust the text in this letterhead.

40. Highlight **Tina Pettle**.

41. Press T, then ↵ when the dialog box appears to change text to graphics.

42. To enlarge the name, press E, + twice, then ↵.

43. With the highlight still on the name, press M, → three times, then ↵ to move it.

44. Using the procedure in step 43, move the next three lines three spaces to the right.

45. Press Esc to return to the LETTERHEAD: Top screen.

Repeating the Design and Making Adjustments on the Bottom

You can repeat part of the design on the bottom of the letterhead. Here you will use only two sizes of graphics and add a message to advertise a specialty.

46. Highlight Bottom of Letterhead, then press ↵.

47. Graphic is highlighted. Press ↵ to select it.

48. Small Staggered is highlighted. Press ↵ to select it.

49. GRAPHICS Hi Res is highlighted. Press ↵ to select it.

50. Highlight DAISIES, then press ↵.

51. Press → to highlight the third graphic, then press the spacebar to erase it.

52. Press → once to highlight the next graphic, then press the spacebar to erase it.

53. Press ↵ to return to the BOTTOM MENU.

54. Message is highlighted. Press ↵ to select it.

55. Highlight VENTURA, then press ↵.

56. SOLID is highlighted. Press ↵ to select it.

57. Type **Weddings** on this line.

58. Press ↵ to begin a new line.

59. Press F3 to change the font from the default font. Choose VENTURA again.

60. Type **Dinners** on this line.

61. Press Esc to return to the BOTTOM MENU.

Now let's adjust those graphics and enlarge the type a little.

62. Highlight Customize on the BOTTOM MENU, then press ↵.

63. Save a temporary copy of your design.

64. The first graphic is highlighted. Press E, + four times, then ↵ to enlarge it.

65. Press A, then V to align this graphic vertically.

66. With the highlight still on this graphic, press M, → twice, then ↵ to move it.

67. Press → twice to highlight the third graphic.

68. Press F, then H to flip this graphic horizontally.

69. Press → once to highlight the last graphic.

70. Press M, ← three times, then ↵ to move this graphic.

71. Press E, + three times, then ↵ to enlarge this graphic.

72. Press A, then V to align this graphic vertically.

73. Press F, then H to flip the graphic horizontally.

How to View Settings

Sometimes when you are making adjustments, you may need to check if the graphics are properly aligned and the same size. View Settings will tell you exactly where your graphic is and how big it is. Let's check the first and last graphic to be sure they are the same size. Your cursor should still be on the far-right graphic.

74. Press V to view the settings. The size of this graphic is 109 by 64.

75. Press ← three times to highlight the far-left graphic.

76. Press V to view this graphic's settings. Its size is 115 by 68.

The graphics are not the same size. Make the right graphic bigger to match the left one. It's against the right margin, so you will have to move it first.

77. Press Esc to return to the CHOOSE COMMANDS menu.

78. Highlight the far right graphic.

79. Press M, ← once, then ↵ to move the graphic.

80. Press E, + once, then ↵ to enlarge the graphic.

81. Press A, then V to align the graphic vertically.

Enlarging Text on the Bottom

Sometimes when you enlarge text, you may have to move the lines at the bottom down to make room to enlarge the top lines.

82. Highlight **Dinners**.

83. Press T, then ↵ when the dialog box appears to change text to graphics.

84. Press E, + twice, then ↵ to enlarge this line.

85. Press A, then H to align the text horizontally.

86. Press M, ↓ once, then ↵ to move the bottom line down.

87. Highlight **Weddings** and repeat steps 84 and 85.

88. Press Esc to return to the BOTTOM MENU.

Add the ruled line and you are finished.

89. Highlight Ruled Line, then press ↵.

90. Select Thin Line.

91. Print and save the sample.

10 *Using Additional Borders, Graphics, and Fonts*

The graphics and fonts that come with The New Print Shop are not always right for the design you are creating. For example, you may be planning an invitation for a barbecue or producing a calendar for a sport such as tennis, cycling, or skiing. You may want a more formal font or a more humorous one. There is additional software you can purchase to create your own collection of graphics, fonts, borders, patterns, and panels.

What's Available in The New Print Shop Graphics Library

The New Print Shop Graphics Library by Brøderbund includes three separate software packages that you can purchase to expand your graphics collection. The Party Edition, the Sampler Edition, and the School & Business Edition each contain additional graphics, fonts, borders, patterns, and panels.

Although these additional graphics and fonts can be used with the skills you have already learned, they can also greatly expand the things you can do with The New Print Shop.

Let's examine a few possibilities.

Additional Black-and-White Individual Graphics

Each edition contains thirty-five black-and-white individual graphics and ten new fonts. Illustrations of these graphics and fonts can be found in Appendix C.

One very interesting and useful graphic from the School & Business Edition appears in Figure 10.1—the empty quote balloon, shown here with the rabbit graphic from the Sampler Edition. The quote balloon can be used as is or flipped horizontally to face the other way. For this example, it was stretched in Customize to surround the message. It can be made larger or smaller to enclose words for a character such as the rabbit or to highlight a saying in a sign or flyer. Here the Large Bottom layout was chosen and the rabbit graphic selected, then the quote graphic was inserted in Customize.

Figure 10.1: *This quote balloon from the School & Business Edition and the rabbit from the Sampler Edition are examples of the individual graphics available in The New Print Shop Graphics Library.*

Additional Borders

Each edition comes with an additional five thin borders to use in your designs. The Sampler Edition and the School & Business Edition also include an extra seven black-and-white wide borders.

The BRIDAL wide border in Figure 10.2 is one of the four wide borders provided in the Party Edition. It is shown here with the beautiful FORMAL font (also available in the Party Edition)—a font that allows you to create some very elegant designs.

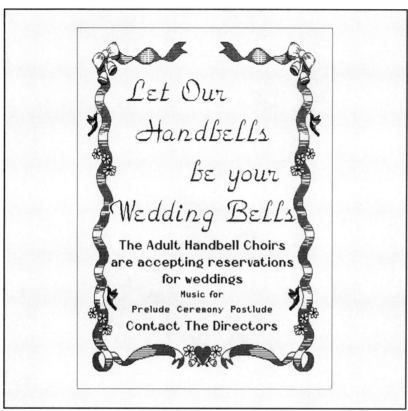

Figure 10.2: The BRIDAL wide border is one of the four wide borders provided in the
Party Edition. It is shown here with the beautiful FORMAL font that is
also available in the Party Edition.

Additional Full Panels

Each edition comes with an additional three horizontal and five vertical black-and-white full panels. These allow you to create a wide variety
of new products. The horizontal full panel SCROLL, shown in Figure 10.3 (available in the Sampler Edition), is just one example of these
new choices. The JOYCE font used in this illustration is also available
in the Sampler Edition.

Figure 10.3: The horizontal full panel SCROLL is an example of the additional black-and-white full panels you can use with The New Print Shop. This panel and the JOYCE font used here are available in the Sampler Edition.

New Patterns Are Also Included

Five patterns for creating tiled designs are included in each edition.

While the patterns can be used for overall designs, they can also be used with a border around the edge or around the inside as shown in Figure 10.4. The inside border used here is the empty box graphic you created with the Graphic Editor in Chapter 8. It was inserted into this flyer as a medium graphic with the Insert command in Customize, then stretched to form the inside border.

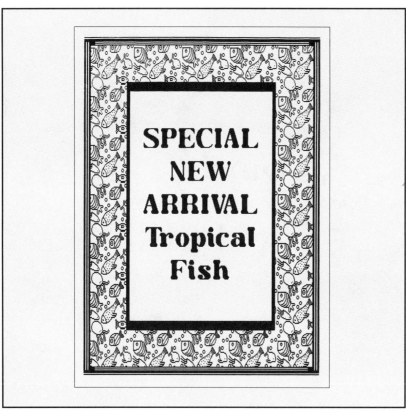

Figure 10.4: The fish pattern, the MULTILINE thin border, and the BRONTE font are all from the Sampler Edition. The inside border is the empty box graphic created in the Graphic Editor and inserted and stretched in Customize.

This fish pattern from the Sampler Edition is a continuous design with no edges. It was used in the Small Frame layout with the MULTILINE thin border and the BRONTE font.

Multicolor Graphics and Panels

In addition to the black-and-white graphics, each edition also contains fifteen individual multicolor graphics, two multicolor wide borders, two multicolor horizontal panels, three multicolor vertical panels, and two multicolor letterhead full panels.

Using the Graphics Library

To use these additional graphics, fonts, and borders with The New Print Shop, you will need to change drives. Let's see how this works.

Using Individual Graphics

When you decide to put graphics into your design, you highlight Graphics from the menu of the project you are working in. It may be from the GREETING CARD: Front menu, the SIGN OR POSTER menu, the LETTERHEAD: Bottom menu, etc.

When you highlight Graphics and press ↵, a screen comes up with the GRAPHICS Hi Res File on it. In most of the examples, you have been using this file, which contains the individual graphics that come with the program. To use the Graphics Library, you do not select this file. Instead, you access the disk containing the extra graphics.

Press F9 to choose the drive that your graphics disk is in. If you are using a hard drive, place the disk in drive A. If you are using two floppy-disk drives, you will have your program disk in drive A and the graphics disk in drive B. If you are using one floppy disk, use the graphics disk instead of your data disk. You will then have a choice of a Hi Res file or a pattern file. Choose the Hi Res file.

If you are using a hard drive, you will find that it is easier and faster to locate the graphics that you want if you keep them on floppies. This is true for fonts and borders also.

Using Additional Fonts

When you select Message or Text in the project you are using, you will get a listing of the fonts in The New Print Shop. At this time you can place your graphics disk in the appropriate drive and again press F9. The menu box on the left of your screen will then display the list of fonts available on this disk.

Using Full Panels

When you choose Full Panel from the GRAPHIC LAYOUT menu and press ↵, you get a list of full panels from the program. Press F9 and change to the drive containing the disk with the additional panels. You will get a list of the full panels on this disk.

Using Thin and Wide Borders

When you select Border in the project that you are working in, a screen appears that gives you a choice between thin and wide borders. At this point press F9 and change to the drive containing the disk with your additional borders. The menu on your screen will then list those new border selections.

Using Additional Patterns

When you highlight Graphics in the project you are working in and press ↵, you get a screen that lists GRAPHICS Hi Res and Original Patterns. At this point press F9 and change drives. You will then have a choice of Hi Res or Patterns from the new disk. Choose Patterns and the new list of patterns will appear on your menu.

Other Software for The New Print Shop

There are many places to find additional software to use with The New Print Shop.

One of the best places to start is by using what you may already have. If you do not have a color printer, you may want to start adding to your graphics collection by converting the multicolor graphics that come with The New Print Shop into black-and-white graphics. If you have the original Print Shop program, the old Print Shop Graphics Library, the original Print Shop Companion or Print Shop compatible graphics collections, you can convert them to use with The New Print Shop.

The conversion process makes a copy of the multicolor or original graphic. You will still have the original to use any time.

Let's convert the multicolor graphics that come with The New Print Shop. Then, if you have other graphics, you may follow instructions in this chapter to convert those also.

Before you begin, format several floppy disks. You will use these to store your converted graphics. It is a good idea to format at least one disk for every disk you intend to convert. Therefore, if the multicolor graphics are on one 3½-inch disk, you will need to format one 3½-inch disk for your new graphics. If the multicolor graphics come on two 5¼-inch disks, you will need to format two 5¼-inch disks. Since you cannot leave the program to format new disks if you do not have enough room, it's wise to always have an extra disk handy. Format one more disk than you think you will need.

The New Print Shop Conversion Utility

The New Print Shop comes with a special utility program to convert graphics from color to black and white. You access this program from your DOS prompt, not from the MAIN MENU. The procedure for this will vary depending on the drive configuration of your computer.

Accessing the Conversion Utility with Floppy-Disk Drives

If you are using a computer that has one or two floppy-disk drives, use the following procedure to access the Conversion Utility:

1. Start your computer as usual.

2. Insert the disk with the Conversion Utility in drive A. If you are using 5¼-inch disks, this will be Data Disk 2. If you are using 3½-inch disks, it will be the Data Disk.

3. At the DOS prompt, type convert and press ↵.

Accessing the Conversion Utility with Hard-Disk Drives

If you are using a computer that has a hard drive, use the following procedure to access the Conversion Utility:

1. Turn on your computer.

2. Change to the subdirectory that contains The New Print Shop. If you did not change the name for the subdirectory during the Install procedure, it will be called NEWPS.

3. *Before* you load The New Print Shop, at the <NEWPS> prompt type convert and press ↵.

Converting Color Graphics

Either of the previous two procedures gives you access to The New Print Shop Conversion Utility and brings up the first screen as shown in Figure 10.5.

Both floppy-disk and hard-disk users can follow steps 4 and 5.

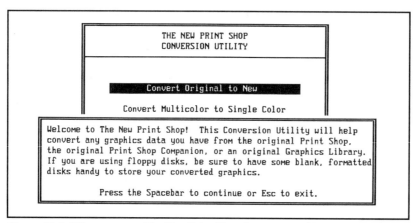

Figure 10.5: When you enter The New Print Shop Conversion Utility, this is the first screen you will see.

4. Press the spacebar to continue.

The Conversion Utility menu (Figure 10.6) now appears on your monitor and gives you the following choices:

Convert Original to New

Convert Multicolor to Single Color

Exit

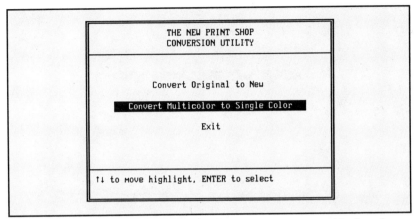

Figure 10.6: The Conversion Utility menu allows you to convert graphics from the original Print Shop program or the multicolor graphics that come with The New Print Shop.

Let's convert the color graphics that come with The New Print Shop program to black and white.

5. Highlight Convert Multicolor to Single Color, then press ↵.

The Color Conversion menu (Figure 10.7) now appears on your screen and offers you the following choices:

Graphics

Full Panels

Wide Borders

Converting Individual Graphics

Although you want to convert all the multicolor graphics to black and white, you must choose one kind of graphic at a time. Graphics means the individual graphics.

In the following procedure you will be asked to place either a source disk or a destination disk into the drive of your computer. The source disk is the one that has the multicolor graphics on it. The destination disk is one of the blank floppy disks you formatted before you started.

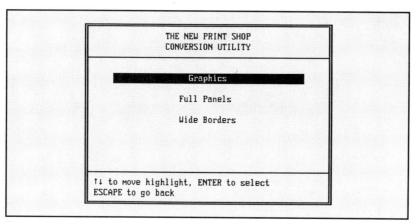

Figure 10.7: *The Color Conversion menu allows you to choose the kind of graphic you wish to convert.*

Using One Floppy-Disk Drive   If you have one floppy disk drive, you can convert the individual graphics with the following procedure:

6. Press ↵ to select Graphics.

You must now identify the drive you will be using for the source disk. The Conversion Utility asks where it should select the files from.

7. Highlight drive A, then press ↵.

The Conversion Utility reads the disk and prints on screen the list of files available.

If you accidentally place the wrong disk in the drive, a dialog box will tell you that there are no files available. Change disks, inserting the correct one in the drive. Press Esc, then repeat step 7. You should now have a list of the files available.

You can use the spacebar to select a file, F1 to select all files, or Esc to go back to the previous screen.

8. Press F1 to select all files.

9. Press F10 to convert the files.

A new screen now requests information about your destination drive. You have already told the program where to find the source, now you must tell it where to put the converted files. With one floppy drive you must use drive A as both the source and the destination.

10. Remove the source disk now and place the destination disk in drive A.

When you follow the next steps, the Conversion Utility places a destination tag on the disk you insert in the destination drive. When you convert the graphics, the Conversion Utility looks for this destination tag and places the graphics on the disk that is tagged. If you leave the source disk in the destination drive and the tag is placed on this disk, the program will write the files on your source disk.

11. Highlight the destination drive, then press ↵.

A message now tells you that there are no more subdirectories.

12. Press F10 to place converted files on the disk in the selected drive.

You will now get a dialog box that says that you cannot convert a color file to a monochrome file without first giving the file a new name. This is a safety feature that keeps you from accidentally destroying the beautiful color file. You must create another file for your newly converted black-and-white graphics. The originals will remain for you to use as color graphics should you need them.

Type in the new file name. You may want to just add **BW** to the end so that you will recognize the color graphic and know that it is now black and white. Adding extra letters sometimes results in an error message. To be safe, you should delete one or two letters from the end of the file and then type **BW**.

13. Backspace to erase the last two letters of the file name.

14. Type **BW** at the end of the file name. (Make the file name one word—do not leave a space or use a dot between the old file name and the **BW**.)

15. Press ↵ to enter the new file name.

A prompt will now ask you to insert the source disk in drive A and press ↵ to continue, or press Esc to cancel the procedure.

16. Remove the destination disk.

17. Insert the source disk, then press ↵.

Prompts will now tell you when to insert either the destination disk or the source disk in the disk drive. You will need to do this disk swapping several times before the conversion is over.

18. Watch the prompts and carefully follow their instructions to place either the destination disk or the source disk in drive A.

Warning: The prompt on your computer screen may come on before the light on the disk drive is out. *Never* remove a disk from the disk drive if the light is on! Wait until the light is out before you remove the disk.

Using Two Floppy-Disk Drives   If you are using two floppy-disk drives, you can convert the individual graphics with the following procedure:

6. Press ↵ to select Graphics.

7. Place the source disk in drive A and the destination disk in drive B.

You must now tell the Conversion Utility where you have placed these disks. First the Conversion Utility asks where it should select the files from.

8. Highlight drive A, then press ↵.

The Conversion Utility reads the disks and prints on screen the list of files available. You can use the spacebar to select a file, F1 to select all the files, or Esc to go back to the previous screen.

9. Press F1 to select all files.

10. Press F10 to convert selected files.

A new screen now requests information about your destination drive.

11. Highlight drive B, then press ↵.

A message now says that there are no more subdirectories.

12. Press F10 to place the new converted files onto the disk in the selected drive.

You will now get a dialog box that tells you that you cannot convert a color file to a monochrome file without first giving the file a new name. This is a safety feature that keeps you from accidentally destroying the beautiful color file. You must create another file for your newly converted black-and-white graphics.

Type in the new file name. You may want to just add **BW** to the end so that you will recognize the color graphic and know that it is now black and white. Adding extra letters sometimes results in an error message. To be safe, you should delete one or two letters from the end of the file and then type **BW**.

13. Backspace to erase the last two letters of the file name.

14. Type **BW** at the end of the file name. Do not leave a space or use a dot between the old filename and the **BW**. Make the file name one word. Press ↵.

When the conversion is completed, you may continue to convert the multicolor full panels.

Using a Hard-Disk Drive and Storing on a Floppy Disk   If you are using a hard disk, there are several ways you can convert these graphics.

- Use drive A with the method for one floppy-disk drive.

- Convert on your hard drive, store on your hard drive, and copy to a floppy later if desired.

- Convert on the hard drive and use drive A as the destination.

Since The New Print Shop multicolor graphics are already on your hard drive, you will use the third choice listed above—convert on hard drive and save on a floppy—for the following example.

    6.   Press ↵ to select Graphics.

You must now identify the drive you will be using for the source disk. When the Conversion Utility asks where it should select the files from,

    7.   Highlight drive C, then press ↵.

You will now get a list of all the directories on drive C. Highlight the one that contains The New Print Shop. If you did not change the Install program, that directory will be called NEWPS.

    8.   Highlight NEWPS, then press ↵.

You will get a list of the files available. There should be only one, COLOR.CNG. You can use the spacebar to select a file, F1 to select all files, or Esc to go back to the previous screen.

    9.   Press F1 to select all files.

    10.   Press F10 to convert selected files.

A new screen now requests information about your destination drive. This time you want to store the converted files on a floppy in drive A.

    11.   Place a formatted blank disk in drive A.

    12.   Select drive A as the destination drive.

A message on the screen says that there are no more subdirectories.

    13.   Press F10 to place the converted files on the disk in the selected drive (drive A).

You will now get a dialog box that tells you that you cannot convert a color file to a monochrome file without first giving the file a new name. This is a safety feature that keeps you from accidentally destroying the color file. It creates a new file for your black-and-white graphic.

You must type in the new file name. You may want to just add **BW** to the end so that you will know that it is now black and white.

14. Backspace to erase the last two letters of the file name.

15. Type **BW** at the end of the file name. Do not leave a space or use a dot between the old file name and the **BW**—make the file name one word. Press ⏎.

The Conversion Utility will write the converted files on your destination disk automatically and quickly. When you are finished converting the individual graphics, you will be returned to the Conversion Utility menu and may continue to convert the full panels.

Converting Color Full Panels to Black and White

When the individual graphics conversion is finished, you will return to the Color Conversion menu (Figure 10.7). You can now convert the full panels and borders the same way you converted the graphics. Let's try the full panels.

Use the same method—for either one disk drive, two disk drives, or a hard-disk drive—that you used to convert the individual graphics.

1. Highlight Convert Full Panels, then press ⏎.

You will now get a new menu that allows you to choose which kind of full panels you want to convert.

Vertical Full Panels

Horizontal Full Panels

Letterhead Full Panels

The Birthday panel is the only color panel included with The New Print Shop. It is a vertical full panel.

2. Highlight Vertical Full Panels, then press ⏎.

You will now go through a procedure similar to the one you used to convert individual graphics. You may go back to that exercise if you need help with some of the steps.

When the conversion is finished, you will return to the Color Conversion menu and not to the Panel Selection menu because there is only one multicolor full panel on the program disk. When you convert disks from one of the Editions of The New Print Shop Graphics Library, you will be returned to the Panel Selection menu to allow you to convert the Horizontal and Letterhead full panels also.

When you are converting full panels from The New Print Shop Graphics Library, keep a pencil and paper handy to record which files you have converted and which you need to convert. It is easy to get lost or confused in this process, and there is no way to check what you've converted until you are done.

Converting Wide Borders

Now let's try to convert some wide borders.

1. On the Color Conversion menu, highlight Wide Borders, then press ↵.

2. Be sure your source disk is in the correct drive.

3. Highlight the drive for the source disk, then press ↵.

You will be told that there are no files. That's because there are no color border files on the program disk.

The conversion process for the color wide borders in all Editions of The New Print Shop Graphics Library is the same as the procedures you have just used for the individual graphics and the full panels.

Exiting the Conversion Utility

To exit the Conversion Utility you must return to the Conversion Utility menu.

4. Press Esc until you return to the Color Conversion menu.

5. Press Esc once more to return to the Conversion Utility menu.

At this point you can exit the program. (If you have the original Print Shop, Print Shop Companion, or any other original Print Shop graphics disks you would like to convert to use with The New Print Shop, do not exit, but proceed to the next section.)

6. Highlight Exit, then press ↵.

7. At the DOS prompt, type PS to get back into The New Print Shop and create something with your converted graphics.

The sample in Figure 10.8 shows one of the new converted graphics, Santa Claus, used in a letterhead for a service organization that has volunteered to help Santa answer his mail. Only three multicolor

Figure 10.8:One of the color graphics that comes on The New Print Shop program disk is used in a letterhead after it is converted.

individual graphics come with The New Print Shop. The cake graphic is illustrated in Chapter 2 and the sale sign is shown in Chapter 4.

Converting Old Print Shop Graphics

Many people who used the old Print Shop had favorite graphics from that program, such as the antique auto, the sunshine, or the borders of little hearts or notes. If you have the old Print Shop, Print Shop Companion, or collections of graphics for the old program, you can convert them into graphics that you can use with The New Print Shop.

The process is quite similar to that used to convert the color graphics. You access the Conversion Utility the same way, or if you are still in the Conversion Utility from the last example, begin at the Conversion Utility menu.

1. Highlight Convert Original to New, then press ↵.

The Original Graphics Conversion menu now appears. You have three choices from this menu:

> Graphics
>
> Borders
>
> Fonts

You can now convert all your favorite graphics, borders, and fonts. Let's choose Graphics for this example.

2. Highlight Graphics, then press ↵.

3. Select the source drive.

4. Press the spacebar to select the files to be converted or press F1 to select all the files.

5. Press F10 to convert the files.

Now you are asked to select the destination drive.

6. Highlight the correct destination drive, then press ↵.

7. Press F10 to place converted files on the destination disk.

8. Convert the borders and fonts the same way.

9. Press Esc to return to the Conversion Utility menu.

10. Highlight Exit, then press ↵.

You will return to the DOS prompt. Type PS to return to The New Print Shop MAIN MENU.

The greeting card in Figure 10.9 shows the antique auto, the sunshine graphic, and one of the thin borders, all graphics from the old Print Shop that were converted in The New Print Shop Conversion Utility. Here these graphics have been combined with the new SIERRA font.

Try combining the old graphics with the new for added variety in the designs you create in all the projects.

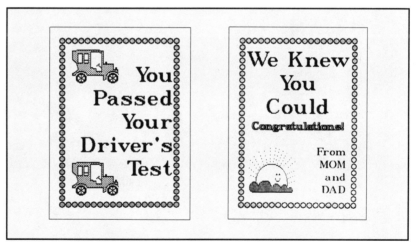

Figure 10.9: This greeting card (front panel on the left, inside panel on the right) shows graphics from the old Print Shop program that have been converted with The New Print Shop Conversion Utility.

11 *Promoting and Organizing Seminars and Conferences*

Now that you've learned how to use each of the projects and features in The New Print Shop, you can integrate them to create all the materials you may need for a particular activity.

Let's start by using The New Print Shop to create materials for a seminar or conference. Of course you will need signs and banners, but what else? Let's look at ways to use all the options available to you.

While you are still planning your conference or seminar, think about what program materials you will need and how The New Print Shop can help you create them.

Using The New Print Shop for Program Materials

Consider the events you are planning for this conference. Is it a one-day workshop, a weekend conference, or will it extend over several days? What activities will be part of the program?

For this example, let's create some materials for a one-day annual conference that brings speakers and participants in from out of town. Since many of them arrive the day before the Saturday conference, you plan an evening social mixer for Friday night. The Saturday conference has an active schedule of general meetings and smaller workshops. It also has a luncheon with a guest speaker, a final awards banquet, and an annual business meeting to officially present the slate of officers for next year. This year the conference will be meeting on a college campus.

Modifying a Graphic for a Logo

Begin by creating a logo which symbolizes the theme for this year's conference. This logo could then be used on all the program materials to provide some unity. This year's theme for our mythical National Association Conference is "Opportunity in the Twenty-First Century."

The Party Edition of The New Print Shop Graphics Library includes an individual black-and-white graphic of the number 21 on a pedestal. You can modify this graphic in the Graphic Editor to use as your logo.

Load this graphic into the Graphic Editor. Erase the design inside the pedestal. With this space blank, you could print the name of the conference here if you use the graphic in the large size on some materials.

You will discover when you erase the inside design that the base is not symmetrical. The right side is longer than the left. You can erase some lines and draw new ones to make the right and left sides the same length. You may also want to adjust the background. The modified graphic should look like the one in Figure 11.1.

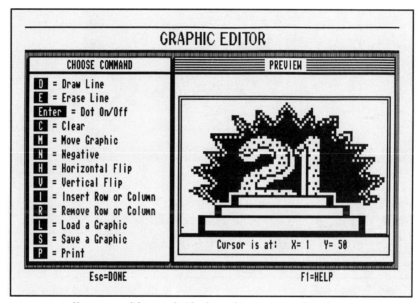

Figure 11.1: You can modify an individual graphic to create a logo for your conference.

Save the modified graphic in a new file in which you will store your creations for this conference. You could call the file NACONF and name the graphic LOGO21.

With just a little adjusting, many small graphics can become customized logos for a particular event.

*U*sing a Daily Calendar for the Program Schedule

Let's create the program schedule for this conference. When participants register, they receive a schedule of events for Saturday. Figure 11.2 shows a sample program created with the daily calendar in the Calendar project.

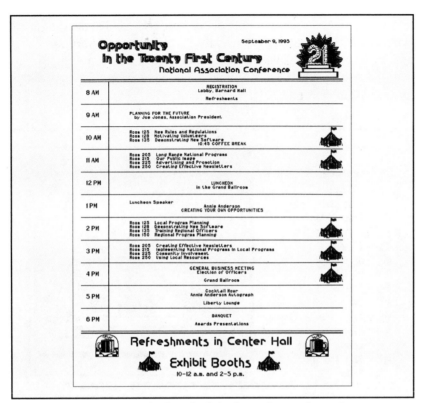

*Figure 11.2: The daily calendar from the Calendar project can be used to create a
    program schedule.*

The top of the calendar is a good place to put the theme or title of this
year's conference, the name of the association sponsoring the conference,
the date, and any identifying logo, such as the logo you created earlier
in the Graphic Editor.

For this sample, the SMALL font was chosen first for the date and
then changed on the next line to SONOMA font in the RAISED style for
the title. On the next line the style was changed to SOLID for the association name. To add the logo graphic to the top of the calendar, the
Right Medium graphic layout was selected, and the graphic LOGO21
chosen from the file NACONF. In Customize the date was moved to the
right and **National Association Conference** was reduced in size.

In the middle of the calendar, the program schedule was organized
hour by hour. Although the talks and workshops can be 50 minutes long
with 10 minutes planned for traveling from one room to another, it isn't

necessary to list this on a program schedule. Using the hour is easier for participants to read and comprehend. If speakers know their time limit, a simple announcement in the opening session can inform everyone of the procedure.

Certain events were emphasized by centering them on the page. Use the F6 key to center your message or place text on the left or right side in each hourly slot.

Graphics can also be used in the hourly entries to call attention to special events. In this example, the tent graphic was used to note the hours that the exhibit booths would be open.

The bottom of the calendar includes additional information about the availability of refreshments and lists the hours for the exhibit booths.

Creating Reception Invitations

Now that you've outlined the events for the conference, plan the materials you will need and use The New Print Shop to create them.

Let's begin with the social event planned for Friday night. You decide to treat it as a reception to welcome the speakers. Although this reception is listed in the advance publicity, you want to call attention to it as a separate function. You decide to include an invitation in the packet the participants receive at registration.

You can create a simple, inexpensive invitation in the Greeting Card project of The New Print Shop. Figure 11.3 shows a sample invitation for the reception. The front was created using the DELICATE wide border from the Sampler Edition of The New Print Shop Graphics Library and the MERCED font in SOLID style from The New Print Shop. The inside was designed by using the CURVY thin border from the Party Edition and reducing some of the type to a smaller size in Customize.

You can photocopy the card on white or colored paper to make as many copies as you need and enclose them in matching envelopes.

Using a Letterhead for the Business Meeting Agenda

To run the business meeting efficiently in the hour you have scheduled, you can create an agenda.

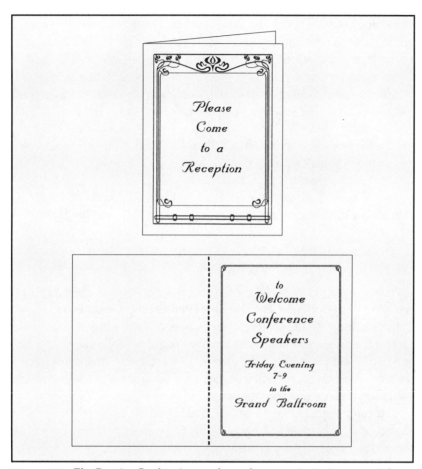

Figure 11.3: The Greeting Card project can be used to create invitations to social events such as a reception.

There is too much information in the agenda to use the large fonts in The New Print Shop, so type this schedule on your word processor and then design a letterhead in The New Print Shop. You could print the letterhead first, then roll the paper back in your printer to print the word processed agenda on the same sheet of paper. Or you can cut out a copy of the agenda and paste it onto the letterhead printout. Photocopy either the printout or pasteup version to create enough copies of the agenda for each participant. Figure 11.4 shows such an agenda.

In the top of this example letterhead we used the logo for the conference and the same font as that in the program schedule, SONOMA.

The date was entered in the TINY font and a thick ruled line selected to finish this design.

Since the bottom of the letterhead was not needed for additional information, the BUSINESS full panel was selected from the School & Business Edition for decoration and to convey the idea that this meeting will be all business.

Creating Program Covers

There may be handout material collected into a program booklet or a report that is traditionally included with the materials. These may require a one-page cover. Here is your opportunity to use the logo in a large

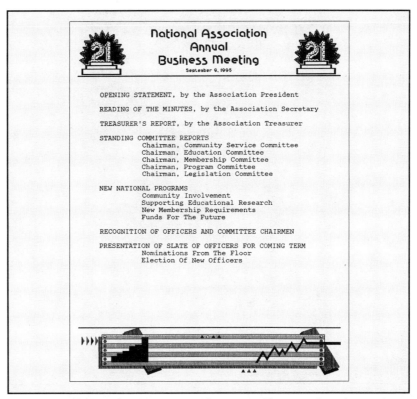

Figure 11.4: The Letterhead project provides a top and bottom and word processing provides the center for this business meeting agenda.

size with the conference name printed in the base. Figure 11.5 shows a program cover created in the Sign project.

You may discover that using the logo in different sizes requires additional modification. To write the conference name in Figure 11.5, it was necessary to remove the lines in the base of the graphic. The first modified graphic, LOGO21, was loaded into the Graphic Editor and the lines were erased. The text was added in the Sign project when the program cover was created.

You could print the same design in a large size for a sign at the registration desk, in the lunchroom, or any other location to identify the parts of the building reserved for your conference.

Figure 11.5: The logo can be printed in the large size for a program cover.

Creating Direction Signs

One of the most popular uses for The New Print Shop is to create the signs and banners that help people find their way around during seminars and conferences. These signs are very easy to create.

Whether your conference is the only one in the building or shares the same building with several other meetings, use distinctive borders to identify the signs for your conference. This can be a wide border or a thin one, but should be the same for all the signs for this conference.

Creating an Arrow Graphic for Direction Signs

Some of the direction signs you create will need an arrow to show which way to go. You can create an arrow graphic (Figure 11.6) easily in The Graphic Editor by following these simple instructions.

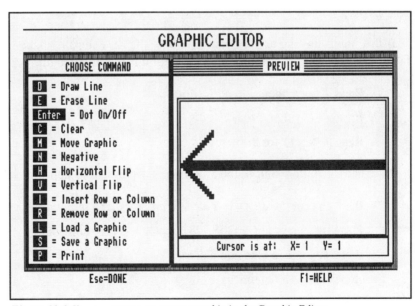

Figure 11.6: You can create an arrow graphic in the Graphic Editor.

1. Highlight the Graphic Editor on the MAIN MENU, then press ↵.

2. Place the cursor at (X=1, Y=24).

3. Press D and then → to draw a line across the screen to the right border (X=88, Y=24).

4. Press ↓ once to move to the next line (Y=25) and then press ← to return to the left border (X=1).

5. Draw two more lines at (Y=26) and (Y=27), then press ↵ to stop drawing.

To create the head of the arrow, you will first erase part of this center line, then draw diagonal lines.

6. Place the cursor at (X=1, Y=24) and press ↵ to delete a dot.

7. Place the cursor at (X=3, Y=23) and press ↵ to add a dot.

8. Press →, ↑, then ↵ to add the next dot.

9. Repeat step 8 ten times.

If this line is as long as you want it, follow the next steps to make it fatter. If you want it longer, repeat step 8 until it is the right length.

10. Press ↓ once, then ↵ to add a dot.

11. Press ↓, ←, then ↵ to add a dot.

12. Repeat step 11 for the rest of the line.

To create the bottom half of the arrow head, follow these steps:

13. Place the cursor at (X=1, Y=27), then press ↵ to remove a dot.

14. Place the cursor at (X=3, Y=28), then press ↵ to add a dot.

15. Press ↓, →, then ↵ to add a dot.

16. Repeat step 15 ten times.

Now make this part of the arrow fatter.

17. Press ↑, then ↵ to add a dot.

18. Press ↑, ←, then ↵ to add a dot.

19. Repeat step 18 for the rest of the line.

When you have finished creating this arrow graphic, store it in the NACONF file and name it H ARROW. Unlike file names that must have only eight letters and no spaces, names of graphics can be longer and can include spaces.

You can flip this graphic to point left or right, but you will have to create a vertical arrow if you need one that points up or down.

Placing Signs at the Entrance

To effectively plan what signs you need and where to place them, walk the route the participants will take. With a notepad and pencil in hand, begin at the parking lot and make notes and designs as you walk along. Do you need a sign on a stake near the curb of the parking lot to tell participants in which building on the campus your conference is located? Walking the route will help you answer questions such as these.

Be sure to use the same border to identify all of your conference signs! Participants may recognize this border from the materials they received in advance, which will make it easier for them to locate the conference building.

On the entrance of the building you need a simple sign such as the one in Figure 11.7 to tell people they have reached the right building. This sign could also tell them where to find the registration desk.

Placing Signs at Intersections

You should consider placing a sign at every intersection to direct people. Figure 11.8 shows what an intersection sign should look like. In Customize the arrow graphic you created in the Graphic Editor was inserted in the sign as a small graphic and then stretched. You would then clone this arrow and flip it horizontally to point to the right for the bottom arrow.

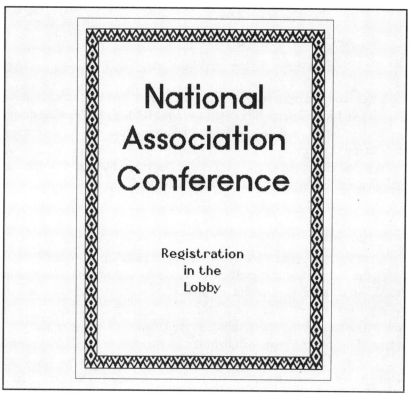

Figure 11.7: Place a sign on the entrance to tell people they have reached the right
building.

Hanging Banners over the Registration Desk

There should be enough signs and banners to tell everyone the location of the registration desk. One horizontal banner over the desk should
give the name of the association or sponsor of the conference. Another
should give this year's title or theme. You can use two single-line horizontal banners or one two-line banner. Put your modified logo on the ends
of the banners.

Listing Workshops or Seminars on a Large Sign

A large sign which lists the workshop topics should hang on the wall
near the registration desk, especially if participants must sign up for these

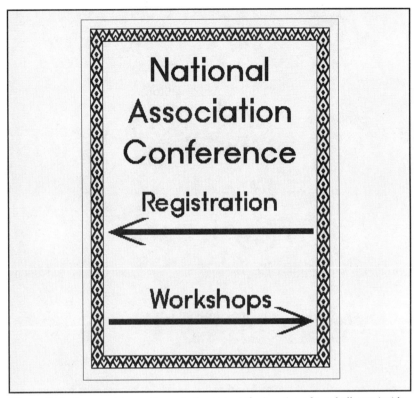

Figure 11.8: At every intersection, whether it is at the junction of two hallways inside or two paths outside, place a direction sign.

workshops when they register. Even if they have preregistered, it's helpful to post such a sign. This could be printed as a large sign in the 2-by-2-sheet size.

Be sure to provide as much information as you can with signs.

Placing Signs at Each Workshop Room

A sign should be placed at the entrance to each workshop room. It should include the distinctive border that identifies your conference, the name of your organization, the title of the workshop, and the name of the person presenting the workshop. Figure 11.9 shows a sample of this sort of sign.

The sign outside the door can be printed in the standard 8½-by-11-inch size and another larger sign can be placed inside the room. Many people

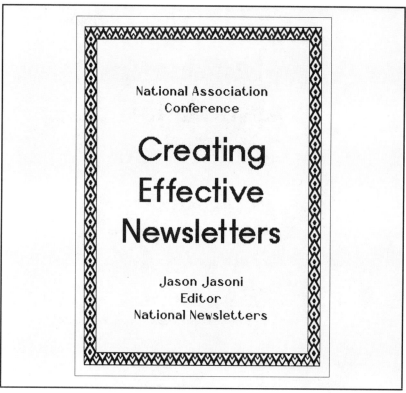

Figure 11.9: The sign outside each workshop room should list the name of your
organization, the title of the workshop, and the name of the person
presenting the workshop.

walk past the sign outside a room and then ask if they are in the right
place. Hang the big sign in the front of the room.

Using Large Signs on Easels

Large signs can be placed on easels when there is no place to hang a
sign or when they need to stand out to attract more attention.

They can be used outside a banquet hall to advertise the guest speaker
or in a lounge for an autograph session. Design the sign in the Sign or
Poster project in either the horizontal or vertical style and then print it in
the 2-by-2-sheet or 3-by-3-sheet size. Glue the sign to cardboard and
place it on an easel.

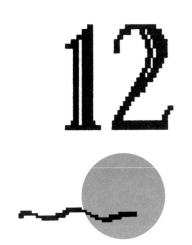

12 *Publicizing and Decorating Suppers and Banquets*

Almost every church or organization uses a supper or breakfast as a fundraiser sometime during the year. For example, the parents of the members of a high school band may hold a chili supper to raise funds to send that band to a parade or football game. A church choir may hold a spaghetti dinner to raise money for new robes. A community service organization may sponsor a pancake breakfast to support a scholarship. Use The New Print Shop to provide invitations, programs, signs, and decorations for fund-raising suppers and banquets.

Creating Signs for Cafeteria-Style Fundraisers

Most of these suppers, dinners, and breakfasts are cafeteria-style meals. They may be held in a school cafeteria or community center where food is served from a counter to people coming through a line.

These fundraisers depend on signs for their success. From the first advertisement to the price list at the cash register, signs are an important part of every fundraiser.

For the following example, let's say that you are one of the parents of a school band member. The school football team is going to a bowl game. The band wants to go along to march in the holiday parade and play at the bowl game. The Band Parents Club decides to have a chili dinner to help raise the money for transportation and lodging. Someone tells the officers of the club that you have The New Print Shop and could make signs for them.

How to Advertise with Signs

The first sign you need to make is one to advertise the event. You decide to create a sign that can be printed in a large size to hang near the school office or the library. You will use the same design for flyers to post throughout the school, in local store windows, and on community center bulletin boards.

Figure 12.1 is an example of this kind of sign. The band graphic in the School & Business Edition of The New Print Shop Graphics Library is perfect. To create this sign, choose the Medium Staggered graphic layout and then use the spacebar to turn off all but the upper-right and lower-left graphics. Use the ROUNDED thin border and the MADERA and SMALL fonts from The New Print Shop for the message. In Customize enlarge and stretch **Chili Supper** and reduce the rest of the words in MADERA font to better contrast the large and small type. Move the top graphic down a bit and reduce the bottom graphic to a smaller size. Then print the sign in different sizes and photocopy 100 small flyers.

Figure 12.1: Design a sign to be printed in different sizes to advertise your fundraiser.

You could also create a banner for the lunch room or other location. Use the same band graphic and the same font whenever possible so that they become identifying symbols for this event.

Displaying the Price of the Meal

When your advertising signs are finished, you can begin creating the signs to be used at the supper. This takes a little advance planning. You may need to talk to the committee members to find out where signs will be most helpful.

You will need to make a sign listing the price of the meals. Figure 12.2 shows how this sign could be designed.

This sign uses the band graphic and the MADERA font that you used in your advertisement, as well as the Small Frame graphic layout. In Customize **Chili Supper** was enlarged and stretched and the other words and prices reduced.

Figure 12.2: A sign with the price of the supper should be placed near the cash register.

Giving Directions with Signs

You may want to move one large sign or banner to the room where the dinner is being held to let people know they are in the right place.

Another sign could be placed on the entrance door and direction signs in the hallways as suggested for conferences in Chapter 11.

You should also post a sign that tells people where the food line starts. Figure 12.3 shows an example of this kind of sign.

The sign in Figure 12.3 uses the CUT CORNERS thin border from the School & Business Edition of The New Print Shop Graphics Library. The sandwich graphic is from the Party Edition and the other three graphics are from the Sampler Edition. The arrow is the one you created in the Graphic Editor in Chapter 11. In Customize the arrow was inserted as a

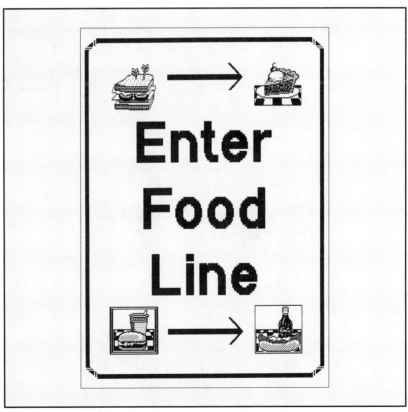

Figure 12.3: Every cafeteria-style supper needs a sign to tell people where to get their food.

small graphic and stretched and flipped horizontally. It was then cloned to create the bottom arrow. Always use a simple font for directions. The ELIOT font from the Sampler Edition, shown in Figure 12.3, is a good choice.

Identifying Beverages with Signs

Whether it's just a matter of specifying which coffee is regular and which is decaffeinated or identifying different beverages in a group, use small signs to do the job. The iced tea sign in Figure 12.4 is a top-fold greeting card with a blank inside. It will stand by itself on the table next to the pitcher or urn containing the beverage. The top-fold card can be printed in regular size or a smaller size.

Posting No Smoking Signs

You may want to have a separate nonsmoking section or limit the entire room to nonsmoking. The School & Business Edition contains a graphic which can be used for a No Smoking sign (Figure 12.5).

Figure 12.4: This top-fold card will stand by itself next to a pitcher or urn to identify its contents.

Figure 12.5: Whether you have a separate nonsmoking section or limit the entire room, create a No Smoking sign.

The MULTILINES thin border from the Sampler Edition was used for the sign in this example. The MADERA font from The New Print Shop was stretched in Customize.

*C*reating Everything You Need for Banquets

Many organizations, especially youth groups such as the 4-H Club and Cub Scouts, hold an awards banquet to present honors to their members. Some organizations hold an annual parent-child banquet. Many of these events use programs and table decorations that you can make with

The New Print Shop. Let's look at some examples of the things The New Print Shop can create for an awards banquet.

Using the Same Design for Invitations and Programs

Both the invitations and the program can be created in the Greeting Card project. Use the same design on the front of the invitation and the program.

Figure 12.6 shows an example of a program for an awards banquet. On the front the FILIGREE wide border from the Sampler Edition surrounds the trophy graphic from the School & Business Edition. The fancy font JOYCE from the Sampler Edition was used to create the text.

Inside, the program lists the order of activities in the same font. The TWISTED thin border is from the School & Business Edition. The trophy graphic is repeated in the Small Corners graphic layout.

Creating Table Decorations

The New Print Shop can help you create some interesting table decorations for an awards banquet, such as place cards, table runners, centerpieces, and place mats.

Using the Name File to Make Place Cards

The top-fold card can be used to create place cards. Figure 12.7 shows a sample place card made with the trophy graphic. The Large Top graphic layout was chosen and then the graphic was moved to the right in Customize. If you don't use a border, you can fold the card any way you want. This place card was printed in 75 percent size and folded as a conventional top-fold card. Then it was cut in half horizontally to create the narrow place card size.

If you want to use the Name File, you must use only one line for the name, as shown in Figure 12.8. The Name File can print the first name or the whole name, but it can print on one line only.

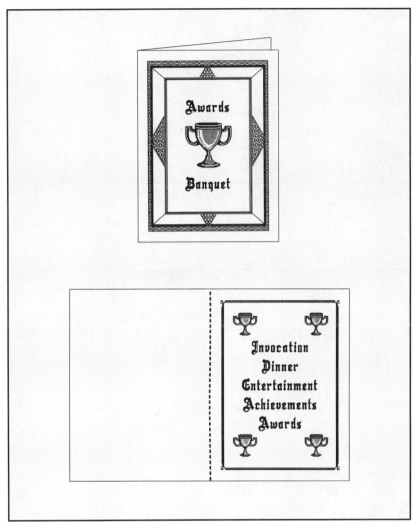

Figure 12.6: Both the invitation and the program for an awards banquet can be created in the Greeting Card project.

Using Banners as Table Runners

Sometimes it is necessary to place special decorations on the head table to reserve it. In The New Print Shop you can create a horizontal banner that can be used as a table runner for the head table.

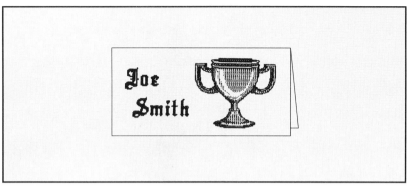

Figure 12.7: The Greeting Card project can be used to create place cards.

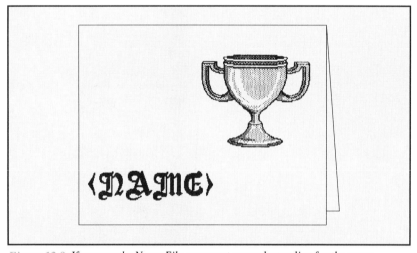

Figure 12.8: If you use the Name File, you must use only one line for the name.

To create the table runner in Figure 12.9, the Banner project was used. The trophy graphic was selected in the Large Graphic Both Ends layout. Then the right-hand graphic was changed to RIBBON (a graphic from The New Print Shop). It was flipped vertically so that the banner could be viewed from either side. If you don't use a message or a trim, only the graphics are printed out. By setting the number of copies to three or more, you will get a continuous printing of the graphics.

Using the Name File to Make Place Mats

Instead of place cards, you could create individual place mats with the Name File. Figure 12.10 shows an example of a place mat that has

Figure 12.9: By selecting only graphics for a horizontal banner you can create a table runner for the head table.

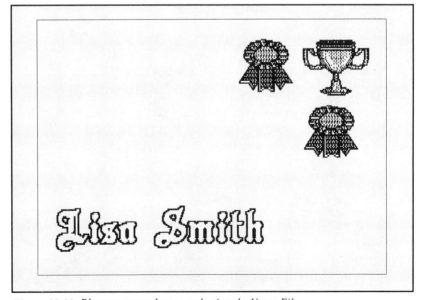

Figure 12.10: Place mats can be created using the Name File.

graphics in the upper-right corner and the name in the lower-left corner. The graphics could be placed on the page in one of the graphic layout choices, then moved in Customize, or you could just as easily insert them in Customize. The JOYCE font from the Sampler Edition was used in the OUTLINE style for the name.

Creating Centerpieces

There are several ways you can use The New Print Shop to create centerpieces for tables.

You can print out individual graphics in Quick Print, or the Greeting Card or Sign projects, depending on the size you need. You can print a front and a back, then cut out the graphics and glue them together to create a two-sided graphic. Before you glue the graphics together, insert an ice cream stick or toothpick between them. Push the stick or toothpick into a Styrofoam base. You could use different size ribbon graphics on a single base to create an attractive centerpiece.

You can also create patterned paper to use in making small centerpieces. Figure 12.11 shows a pattern that uses the ribbon and trophy graphics. You could use this paper to cover an empty frozen juice can (or any small can) to create a vase for flowers. You could also use this paper to make nut cups.

Using Large Graphics for Wall Decorations

Large graphics from the Sign project or Banner project can be cut out and used to decorate walls and windows. Use the instructions given in Chapter 2 to stretch a graphic across a full page and print it in a larger size if you need larger graphics for wall decorations.

Creating the Certificates or Awards

You cannot have an awards banquet without awards, and The New Print Shop can print them for you. Follow the instructions given in Chapter 2 to create the certificates. Also check the directions given in Chapter 6 for placing the names on them automatically.

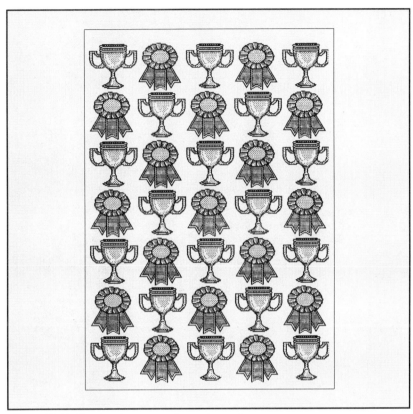

Figure 12.11: Patterned paper can be used to make a vase or nut cup.

13 *Advertising and Improving Sales and Bazaars*

Use The New Print Shop to create advertising and information signs for sales and bazaars. You can make sale invitations, design unique graphics, make top-fold business cards, print large window and door signs, use banners for directions, and promote demonstrations.

Using The New Print Shop to Make Advertisements

You can use the Greeting Card and Sign projects to create unique advertising for sales and bazaars.

Designing a Preview Sale Invitation

You may want to use the Greeting Card project to create invitations to special previews or advance sale days. A card-size invitation may catch a reader's attention where an advertising flyer may be considered junk mail. Figure 13.1 shows an example of an invitation to a fall preview sale for preferred customers.

The OAK full panel was used on the front of this invitation and the fall leaves theme was continued on the inside with a new grouping of modified graphics. The SUTTER font was chosen for the text, and

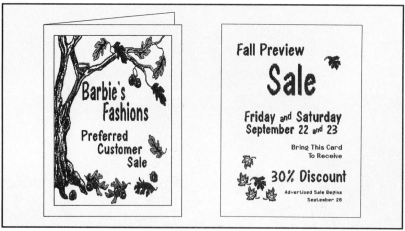

Figure 13.1: The Greeting Card project can be used to create an invitation to a preview sale for preferred customers.

Customize was used to stretch **Barbie's Fashions** and reduce **Preferred Customer Sale**. Since the SUTTER font does not include the & sign, the word **and** is printed on the diagonal when you try to use the ampersand, as shown inside this card.

Grouping Graphics

There may be times when you need to do more to a graphic than just erase part of it or add a few lines. Perhaps you want to take part of a graphic and rearrange it into another grouping. In Figure 13.1 the design on the inside was created by grouping several versions of the LEAVES multicolor graphic from the School & Business Edition.

Since the front of the card was printed in monochrome, the multicolor small graphic was first converted to black and white.

Speedy Erasing

There is a faster way to erase part of a graphic than the method you learned in Chapter 8. In that chapter you were warned that you could lose part of your image if you accidentally moved it off your screen. You can, therefore, deliberately move it off your screen to erase it.

To create the graphics for the new grouping in Figure 13.1, the graphic LEAVES was loaded into the Graphic Editor and the oak leaf was erased by moving the whole image to the right until part of the oak leaf was off the screen and the tip of the maple leaf was at the edge. The image was then moved up until the top of the oak leaf was off the screen (Figure 13.2). This left only a small portion to be erased the conventional way with the Erase Line command.

Storing Multiple Versions

To create several versions of the maple leaf, it was moved to different places on the screen and then saved each time as a new graphic. Then the maple leaf was flipped vertically, and this image was saved as a new graphic also.

After the screen was cleared, the original graphic LEAVES was loaded again, and this time the maple leaf was removed to create an oak leaf graphic.

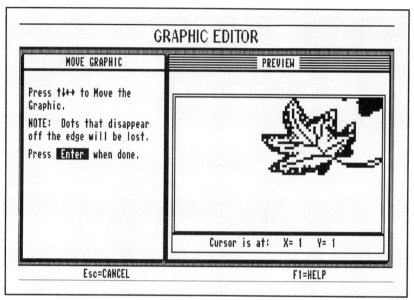

Figure 13.2: To erase part of a graphic quickly, you can move it off the screen.

The new grouping was created by entering the original graphic LEAVES in the SMALL CORNERS layout. The upper-right graphic was changed to the oak leaf graphic and the upper-left and lower-right graphics were turned off with the spacebar. The additional new graphics were placed around the lower-left graphic by using the Insert command in Customize.

Making Folded Business Cards

Use the Greeting Card project to create folded business cards. When printed in a smaller size, top-fold cards are similar to conventional business cards, but can include more information. A single card can be created with The New Print Shop and then photocopied to provide large quantities.

Exhibitors at craft fairs and bazaars can use folded business cards at their booths to advertise their goods (see Figure 13.3). Remember, if you are planning to reduce your card 50 percent or more, you may need to use only large fonts in your design. SMALL and TINY fonts become very hard to read when they are reduced.

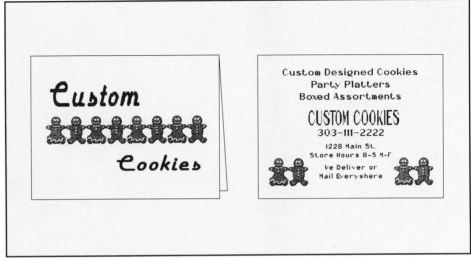

Figure 13.3: *A top-fold Greeting Card can be used as a folded business card to be distributed at booths in a fair, exhibit, or bazaar.*

Using Window and Door Signs

Remember windows and doors as locations for oversize signs. The New Print Shop can create a sign that will cover an entire door or window. Signs on entrance doors can advertise a sale, and signs on inside doors can call attention to items in other locations.

Using The New Print Shop to Make Information Signs

The New Print Shop lets you create maps, direction signs, and events schedules to help make your bazaar or sale run smoothly.

Using Quick Print to Create a Map

Customers attending a large bazaar in a huge hall could use a map to find their way to specific booths. Use Quick Print to print the names of the booths, then cut out the names and paste them on a sheet of paper to indicate the location of the booths. You can then photocopy this sheet to provide maps.

Using Horizontal Banners as Direction Signs

Horizontal banners can be used as direction signs in a large room if you need to point the way to the cash registers, restrooms, refreshments, etc. Use the Banner project, and place the arrow graphic on either the left or right side of the banner.

Suspending Vertical Banners with Helium Balloons

If you need to locate a demonstration stage in the center of a large hall, call attention to the cash registers, or just provide decorations, you may want to consider hanging vertical banners from the ceiling. You can fasten the vertical banners to helium-filled balloons and let the balloons rise to the ceiling. If you have a long or heavy banner, use one very large balloon or several smaller balloons.

Creating a Calendar of Special Events

Perhaps you are featuring demonstrations of some crafts or products as part of the promotion for your bazaar. Create a calendar listing the times for these demonstrations, print it in a large size, and post it near the entrance or in a window. Figure 13.4 shows a calendar for a country crafts fair.

This example also demonstrates a problem with centering text when designing both the daily and weekly calendars in the Calendar Project. The text on the top and bottom of the calendar are centered horizontally between both edges of the paper. The text in the hourly slots is centered in the slot space and not centered on the page. To avoid an overall design that looks off-center, use another alignment in either the top or middle as in the program schedule example in Chapter 11. If you are planning to center the hourly slots, use a left or right alignment for the top and bottom. If you use a centered top and bottom, use a left or right alignment in the hourly entries.

Use type size and graphics to call attention to certain information and add visual interest to the calendar. You can change from small to large type with the F5 key.

In Figure 13.4, the multicolor graphic CORNERPIECE, the full panel TUCSON, and the HARDY font from the Sampler edition were chosen for the top and bottom of the calendar. Small graphics were chosen from all of the different software packages.

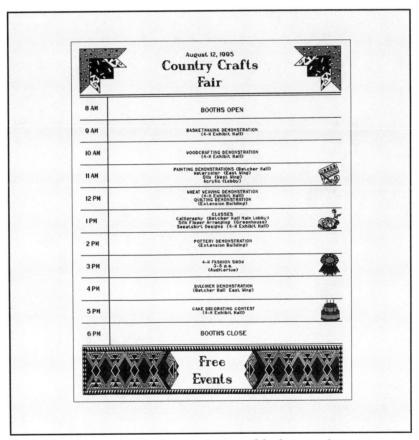

Figure 13.4: Create a calendar that lists the times of the demonstrations at your bazaar.

14 Expanding Your Possibilities with Printers and Photocopiers

The kind of printer, ribbons, and paper you choose all add to the products you can create with The New Print Shop. With a photocopy machine you can expand the capabilities of The New Print Shop even further.

Choosing Printers for The New Print Shop

The appearance of the products you create with The New Print Shop will vary depending on the printer you use. You can use a 9- or 24-pin dot-matrix printer, color printer, or laser printer.

Dot-Matrix Printers

One of the most popular printers for The New Print Shop is the dot-matrix printer with a tractor feed for continuous feed paper. These printers produce long strips for horizontal and vertical banners and extra large signs.

While single-sheet printers produce greeting cards, letterheads, and the standard 8½-by-11-inch flyers and calendars, you will need to assemble individual sheets of paper to create large signs and banners.

Laser Printers

The New Print Shop supports the Hewlett-Packard LaserJet, the IBM Personal Pageprinter and 100 percent compatibles. To use a laser printer, select Setup from the MAIN MENU and choose your printer from the list of printers that the program supports.

Color Printers

If your system includes a color printer, at least 640K of RAM, and a hard disk, you can print in color with The New Print Shop. To preview your projects on screen in color, you will need an EGA card with 256K and an EGA monitor.

When you are set up for color, you can preview in color from any of the project menus by pressing Alt-F10 instead of F10.

Using Colored Ribbons

Ribbons are available in a wide range of colors for most monochrome printers. So even if you do not have a color printer, you can print a color other than black by placing a colored ribbon in your printer.

Using a colored ribbon with colored paper gives the illusion of color printing although it is still monochrome printing.

Selecting Special Paper

You can also use colored paper to create your products in The New Print Shop. Many beautiful colors are available in single sheets or continuous feed paper.

Continuous feed paper is available in bright or pastel colors. The bright colors are red, green, yellow and blue. Pastel shades of pink, cream, light blue, and light green are also available. There is even a paper that resembles parchment for your certificates. You can purchase this colored paper in individual colors or in assortments of colors.

Matching envelopes are available in a business size for your letterhead products, a banner size for mailing your banners, and a greeting card size.

Banner paper is also available. This paper comes in a continuous sheet that does not have perforations. You can cut it to the size you need and not worry about your large signs or banners tearing at the perforations. Some banner paper has illustrations printed along the edges.

Most of these papers are available in stationary or business supply stores or by mail from discount computer supply companies.

Using Heat-Transfer Ribbons

By using a heat-transfer ribbon, you can create designs with The New Print Shop that can be ironed onto any fabric. Replace the printer ribbon with the heat-transfer ribbon. Use the Enhanced Final Quality and the Dark contrast print setting.

If you have letters or words in your design, use the Print Backwards option on the print menu.

You can use any paper, but an erasable bond typewriter paper will improve the final transfer.

To iron your design onto your fabric, first place a piece of aluminum foil on your ironing board to protect it from heat and ink. Then put the fabric on top of the foil. Center the printed transfer design ink-side down on the fabric. Place two pieces of blank paper on top of the design to absorb some of the ink and help avoid scorching. Set your dry iron (do not use steam) at the cotton heat setting and allow it to preheat for at least five minutes. Place the iron firmly on top of the papers and slowly move it back and forth for 30 seconds. Work on small sections at a time. If your design is very large, cut it into smaller sections and iron them separately. Be careful not to let your paper slide or the image may smear.

It's a good idea to practice ironing a small heat-transfer design before you attempt a large one. As with any craft, using heat-transfer ribbons with fabric requires practice.

Be sure to remove your heat-transfer ribbon from the printer when you are finished using it. It should not be used for regular printing because it could damage your print head. Store it in a reclosable plastic bag to keep it from drying out until you need it again.

Experimenting with Contrast

To understand the contrast control on the print menus, create samples to keep in a notebook for handy reference. Select one of the signs that you have created in the Sign project and print that sign eight times, once with each of the following print quality and contrast settings:

Draft Quality	Dark Contrast
Draft Quality	Medium Contrast
Draft Quality	Light Contrast
Draft Quality	Very Light Contrast

Enhanced Final Quality	Dark Contrast
Enhanced Final Quality	Medium Contrast
Enhanced Final Quality	Light Contrast
Enhanced Final Quality	Very Light Contrast

Photocopying Printouts

With a photocopy machine, you can print hundreds of copies of your printouts, print in colored ink on colored paper, use a cut-and-paste layout, enlarge or reduce Quick Print, and reduce signs and calendars.

Using a Photocopier for Mass Production

Whenever you need many copies of a product you design with The New Print Shop, such as invitations or flyers, create a master copy with your printer and then photocopy it to produce the quantity needed. A photocopier can produce the large numbers you need much faster and cheaper than your printer.

Photocopying with Colored Ink and Colored Paper

If you do not have colored ribbons or colored paper for your computer printer, you can get colored copies by photocopying in a colored ink on colored paper. Although you can get colored paper at any copy shop, you may want to check in advance to see if there are any restrictions on the use of colored inks.

Using a Cut-and-Paste Layout with a Photocopier

If you want to add word processed text to the center of the letterhead as suggested for the business agenda in Chapter 11, or create a design beyond the capabilities of The New Print Shop such as the map suggested in Chapter 13, create a cut-and-paste layout to photocopy.

Perhaps you need a sign to direct people down a flight of stairs. You can print out the arrow graphic and paste it in a diagonal position on a sign to indicate the proper direction. Photocopy the layout to produce a new sign.

Using a Photocopier with Quick Print

Using Quick Print and a photocopy machine, you can create many additional products, such as a cut-and-paste layout from Quick Print type and graphics or multiple copies of a line of type or graphic for a bulletin board display. And you can enlarge or reduce the Quick Print type and graphics.

Using a Photocopier for Reduction

The ability to enlarge or reduce printouts with a photocopier gives you additional opportunities to modify your products.

Creating Smaller Signs

Although you can print smaller Greeting Cards, you can only print larger signs and posters. Perhaps you need a small sign. Create the sign in the Sign Project and then photocopy it using an appropriate reduction for one or more copies.

Creating Smaller Calendars

Like the Sign Project, the Calendar Project only prints out in large sizes. Perhaps you need a small calendar to use individually or include in another publication such as a newsletter. You can use the reduction capabilities of a good photocopy machine to create smaller sizes.

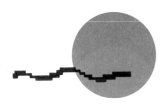

Getting Started with The New Print Shop

It is very easy to get started with The New Print Shop on a computer that has either a floppy-disk drive or hard-disk drive.

Requirements

To run The New Print Shop, you need the following:

An IBM PC, PC/XT, PC/AT, PS/2 or PC compatible computer

512K of memory

DOS (version 2.1 or higher)

A graphics card and monitor (color or monochrome)

A printer (Check the back of the software box for the current list of printers supported.)

To run The New Print Shop with a color printer you need:

640K of memory

A hard disk

A color printer

The New Print Shop consists of either three 5¼-inch disks, which include the following:

The New Print Shop Program Disk

Data Disk 1 (which includes fonts and graphics)

Data Disk 2 (which includes multicolor graphics, full panels, and the Conversion Utility)

or two 3½-inch disks, as listed here:

The New Print Shop Program Disk

Data Disk

Although The New Print Shop will operate with a Microsoft mouse, one is not needed.

Making Backup Copies of the Disks

The first thing you should do is make backup copies of the disks that come with the program. The New Print Shop is not copy protected and you can make copies with the DISKCOPY command. You will need three 5¼-inch blank disks or two 3½-inch blank disks.

Even if you have a hard disk, you may want the security of having an extra set of backup disks.

1. Start computer as usual.

2. With your DOS disk in drive A and a new blank disk in B, type DISKCOPY A: B: then press ⏎.

3. When the message on your screen requests that you insert the source disk in drive A, remove the DOS disk and place The New Print Shop Program Disk in drive A.

4. With The New Print Shop Program Disk in drive A and a new blank disk in drive B, press any key.

5. When the copying is complete (be sure the disk light is out), remove the disk from drive B and label it (with a felt tip marker) The New Print Shop Backup.

6. When asked if you want to copy another disk, type Y.

7. Repeat the previous steps to copy the remaining disks.

8. Keep the original disks in a safe place, and use the backup disks in your computer.

Formatting Data Disks

You will need to format data disks before you enter the program because you cannot format them while using The New Print Shop. If you don't have sufficient storage room available when you try to save a design on a floppy, you may lose your creation because you have no place to put it. Have at least three to five formatted disks handy at any one time. Even though you have a hard disk, you will want to store many of your creations on floppy disks.

You may want to have a filing system for these data disks. You could organize the data according to an activity such as a conference and have all the data for that on one disk. Or you could place all like products, such as all calendars, on one disk.

If you have a floppy-drive system, place your DOS disk in drive A and continue with the following steps. If you have a hard disk, change to the directory that contains DOS.

1. From the DOS prompt, type FORMAT B: and press ↵.

2. When prompted, insert the new diskette into drive B, then press ↵.

3. When the formatting is complete, remove the disk and place a label on it.

4. When asked if you want to format another disk, type Y and format additional disks.

If you follow a policy of attaching labels only to formatted disks, you will be able to tell which disks are formatted. When you use a formatted disk, enter the information on the label with a felt-tip pen.

Installing the Program on a Hard Disk

Hard-disk users can follow this procedure for installing The New Print Shop on their computer.

1. Start your computer.

2. Place The New Print Shop Program Disk in drive A.

3. The DOS prompt should be A>. If it is not, type A: and press ↵.

4. Type Install then press ↵.

You can now follow the installation directions on your screen. If you want to choose the default setting, just press ↵. If you want to select a different option, just choose the number of that option from the list that appears on screen and type that number. You do not have to press ↵ after you type the alternate selection.

5. For disk drive configuration, select the right number from the list on the screen.

The installation program will automatically create a subdirectory called NEWPS and place The New Print Shop in it. If you want to call the subdirectory something else, you can do so at this point. If you already have the old Print Shop on your hard disk and wish to keep it there, be sure to store the new version in another subdirectory. If there is no reason to reject NEWPS as the subdirectory, use this name, because instructions in this book and in the documentation will refer to it.

Starting the Program

When you have finished installing the program on your hard disk you can begin using it. If you are using a floppy-disk system, remember to use the backup copies you have just created.

Using a Floppy Disk System

If you have a floppy disk system, start The New Print Shop this way:

1. Turn on your computer with the DOS disk in drive A.

2. When you see the A> prompt, replace the DOS disk in drive A with the backup copy of The New Print Shop Program Disk. If you have two disk drives, place Data Disk 1 in drive B.

3. Type PS then press ↵.

The New Print Shop title screen will be displayed on your monitor while the program is loading. When the MAIN MENU appears, you can begin using The New Print Shop.

Using a Hard Disk System

If you have a hard disk system, you can start The New Print Shop by following these steps:

1. Turn on your computer.

2. At the C> prompt, type CD\NEWPS then press ↵ to change to the NEWPS subdirectory.

3. Type PS then press ↵.

When the MAIN MENU appears, you may begin using The New Print Shop.

Setting Up Your Printer

Before you create anything, you will need to set up the printer so that you can print out your product when you finish it.

1. On The MAIN MENU, press ↓ several times to highlight Setup, then press ↵.

The SETUP MENU (Figure A.1) will appear on your screen. The list of choices appears in the box on the left and the CURRENT SETUP appears in the box on the right. The default setting is for an Epson FX 80/85/86 and a parallel port 1 (LPT1). If this is your system, you do not

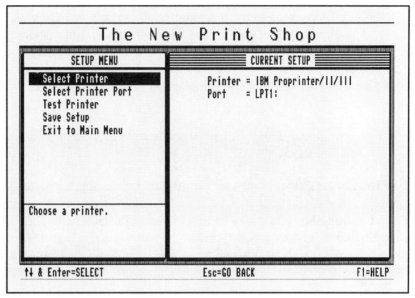

Figure A.1: The SETUP MENU

need to select a printer or printer port, but can proceed to the directions for testing your printer.

If you have a different printer, follow these steps:

2. Highlight Select Printer, then press ↵.

3. Use the arrow keys to highlight your printer on the list of compatible printers that appears in the box at the right of the screen. Press ↵ to select it.

4. Highlight Select Printer Port on the SETUP MENU, then press ↵.

5. Highlight your printer port on the list that appears. The LPT (1 and 2) ports are parallel ports and the COM (1 and 2) are serial ports. (If you are not sure what you have, consult your printer manual.) Press ↵ to select it.

6. Turn on your printer.

7. Highlight Test Printer on the SETUP MENU, then press ↵.

If everything is set correctly, your printer will immediately print the message "Welcome to The Print Shop." If you do not get this response, carefully check the previous procedure. You may need to check the documentation for The New Print Shop or the instruction manuals for both your computer and printer to be sure you have selected the correct settings.

8. Highlight Save Setup, then press ↵ to save your settings and return to the MAIN MENU.

If you choose Exit to Main Menu instead of Save Setup, the settings you selected will only apply to the current session. Next time you use The New Print Shop you will need to set them again. Be sure to choose Save Setup to keep the settings recorded for future use. You can always change them, if you should change equipment, by highlighting Setup on the MAIN MENU.

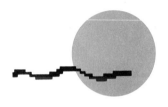

Sizes for Greeting Cards

The New Print Shop

MAIN MENU

Greeting Card
Sign or Poster
Letterhead
Banner

Full Size (100%)

Large (80%)

Medium (75%)

Small (67%)

Tiny (50%)

Very Tiny (33%)

Additional Fonts,
Patterns, and Graphics

FONTS FROM
THE SAMPLER EDITION

BRONTE
ABCDEFGHIJKLMNOPQRSTUVWXYZ
abcdefghijklmnopqrstuvwxyz 1234567890

ELIOT
ABCDEFGHIJKLMNOPQRSTUVWXYZ
abcdefghijklmnopqrstuvwxyz 1234567890

HARDY
ABCDEFGHIJKLMNOPQRSTUVWXYZ
abcdefghijklmnopqrstuvwxyz 1234567890

HUGO
ABCDEFGHIJKLMNOPQRSTUVWXYZ
abcdefghijklmnopqrstuvwxyz 1234567890

JOYCE
ABCDEFGHIJKLMNOPQRSTUVWXYZ
abcdefghijklmnopqrstuvwxyz 1234567890

POE
ABCDEFGHIJKLMNOPQRSTUVWXYZ
abcdefghijklmnopqrstuvwxyz 1234567890

SULLIVAN
ABCDEFGHIJKLM NOPQRSTUVWXYZ
abcdefghijklmnop qrstuvwxyz 1234567890

THOREAU
ABCDEFGHIJKLMNOPQRSTUVWXYZ
abcdefghijklmnopqrstuvwxyz 1234567890

TWAIN
ABCDEFGHIJKLMNOPQRSTUVWXYZ
abcdefghijklmnopq rstuvwxyz 1234567890

WILDE
ABCDEFGHIJKLMNOPQRSTU VWXYZ
abcdefghijklmnopqrstuvwxyz 1234567890

FONTS FROM
THE PARTY EDITION

BALLOONS
ABCDEFGHIJ KLMNOPQRSTUVWXYZ
abcdefghij klmnopqrstu vwxyz 1234567890

BRUSH
ABCDEFGHIJKLMNOPQRSTUVWXYZ
abcdefghijklmnopqrstuvwxyz 1234567890

CANDLES
ABCDEFGHIJKLMNOPQRSTUVWXYZ
abcdefghijklmnopqrstuvwxyz 1234567890

DOTS
ABCDEFGHIJKLMNOPQRSTUVWXYZ
abcdefghijklmnopqrstuvwxyz 1234567890

EASTERN
ABCDEFGHIJKLMNOPQRSTUVWXYZ
abcdefghijklmnopqrstuvwxyz 1234567890

FORMAL
ABCDEFGHIJKLMNOPQRSTUVWXYZ
abcdefghijklmnopqrstuvwxyz 1234567890

PARTY
ABCDEFGHIJKLMNOPQRSTUVWXYZ 12345
67890

PRESENTS
ABCDEFGHIJKLMNOPQRSTUVWXYZ
abcdefghijklmnopqrstuvwxyz 1234567890

SHOWER
ABCDEFGHIJKLMNOPQRSTUVWXYZ
abcdefghijklmnopqrstuvwxyz
1234567890

WESTERN
ABCDEFGHIJKLMNOPQRSTUVWXYZ
abcdefghijklmnopqrstuvwxyz 1234567890

FONTS FROM
THE SCHOOL & BUSINESS EDITION

APPLE
ABCDEFGHIJKLMNOPQRSTUVWXYZ
abcdefghijklmnopqrstuvwxyz
1234567890

BLIPPO
ABCDEFGHIJKLMNOPQRSTUVWXYZ
abcdefghijklmnopqrstuvwxyz 1234567890

CHILDREN
ABCDEFGHIJKLMNOPQRSTUVWXYZ
abcdefghijklmnopqrstuvwxyz 1234567890

CLASSIC
ABCDEFGHIJKLMNOPQRSTUVWXYZ
abcdefghijklmnopqrstuvwxyz 1234567890

COLORADO
ABCDEFGHIJKLMNOPQRSTUVWXYZ
abcdefghijklmnopqrstuvwxyz 1234567890

DIGITAL
ABCDEFGHIJKLMNOPQRSTUVWXYZ
abcdefghijklmnopqrstuvwxyz 1234567890

OCTOPUS
ABCDEFGHIJKLMNOPQRSTUVWXYZ
abcdefghijklmnopqrstuvwxyz 1234567890

PARISIAN
ABCDEFGHIJKLMNOPQRSTUVWXYZ
abcdefghijklmnopqrstuvwxyz 1234567890

RESUME
ABCDEFGHIJKLMNOPQRSTUVWXYZ
abcdefghijklmnopqrstuvwxyz 1234567890

STENCIL
ABCDEFGHIJKLMNOPQRSTUVWXYZ
abcdefghijklmnopqrstuvwxyz 1234567890

PATTERNS FROM
THE SAMPLER EDITION

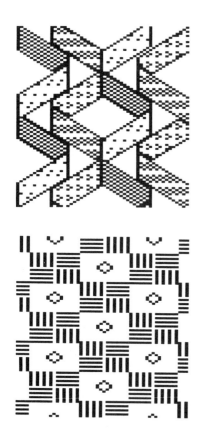

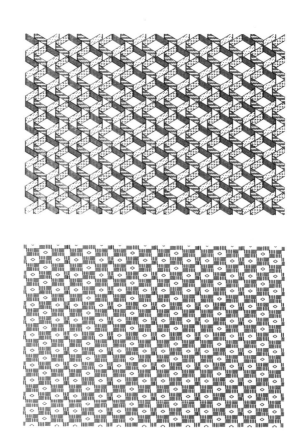

PATTERNS FROM
THE PARTY EDITION

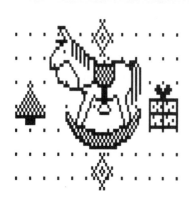

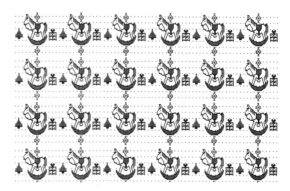

PATTERNS FROM
THE SCHOOL & BUSINESS EDITION

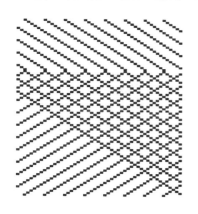

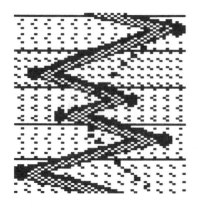

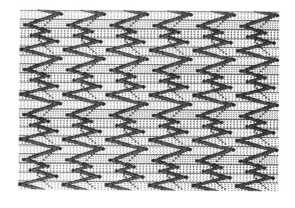

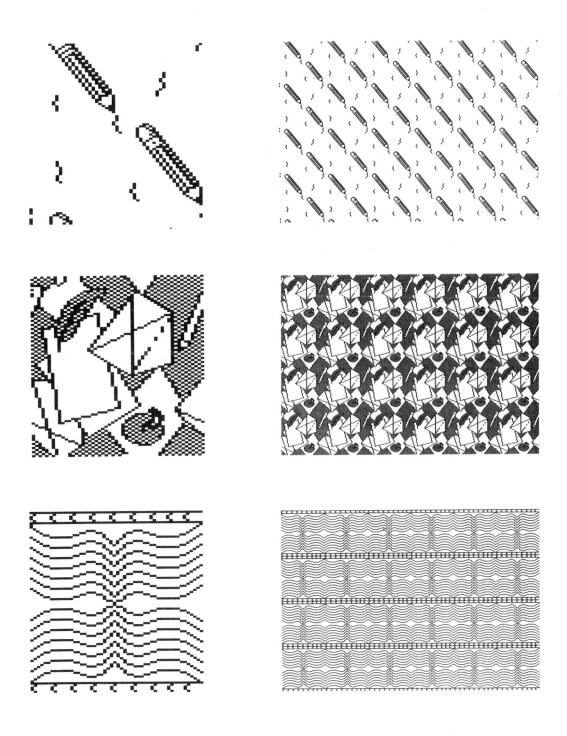

GRAPHICS FROM THE SAMPLER EDITION

GRAPHICS FROM THE PARTY EDITION

GRAPHICS FROM
THE SCHOOL & BUSINESS EDITION

Index

SYBEX®

TO JOIN THE SYBEX MAILING LIST OR ORDER BOOKS
PLEASE COMPLETE THIS FORM

NAME _____ COMPANY _____

STREET _____ CITY _____

STATE _____ ZIP _____

☐ PLEASE MAIL ME MORE INFORMATION ABOUT **SYBEX** TITLES

ORDER FORM (There is no obligation to order)

PLEASE SEND ME THE FOLLOWING:

TITLE	QTY	PRICE
_____	____	____
_____	____	____
_____	____	____
_____	____	____

TOTAL BOOK ORDER _____ $_____

CUSTOMER SIGNATURE _____

SHIPPING AND HANDLING PLEASE ADD $2.00
PER BOOK VIA UPS _____

FOR OVERSEAS SURFACE ADD $5.25 PER
BOOK PLUS $4.40 REGISTRATION FEE _____

FOR OVERSEAS AIRMAIL ADD $18.25 PER
BOOK PLUS $4.40 REGISTRATION FEE _____

CALIFORNIA RESIDENTS PLEASE ADD
APPLICABLE SALES TAX _____

TOTAL AMOUNT PAYABLE _____

☐ CHECK ENCLOSED   ☐ VISA
☐ MASTERCARD   ☐ AMERICAN EXPRESS

ACCOUNT NUMBER _____

EXPIR. DATE _____ DAYTIME PHONE _____

CHECK AREA OF COMPUTER INTEREST:

☐ BUSINESS SOFTWARE

☐ TECHNICAL PROGRAMMING

☐ OTHER: _____

THE FACTOR THAT WAS MOST IMPORTANT IN
YOUR SELECTION:

☐ THE SYBEX NAME

☐ QUALITY

☐ PRICE

☐ EXTRA FEATURES

☐ COMPREHENSIVENESS

☐ CLEAR WRITING

☐ OTHER _____

OTHER COMPUTER TITLES YOU WOULD LIKE
TO SEE IN PRINT:

_____

_____

OCCUPATION

☐ PROGRAMMER   ☐ TEACHER

☐ SENIOR EXECUTIVE   ☐ HOMEMAKER

☐ COMPUTER CONSULTANT   ☐ RETIRED

☐ SUPERVISOR   ☐ STUDENT

☐ MIDDLE MANAGEMENT   ☐ OTHER:

☐ ENGINEER/TECHNICAL   _____

☐ CLERICAL/SERVICE

☐ BUSINESS OWNER/SELF EMPLOYED

CHECK YOUR LEVEL OF COMPUTER USE

☐ NEW TO COMPUTERS

☐ INFREQUENT COMPUTER USER

☐ FREQUENT USER OF ONE SOFTWARE

   PACKAGE:

   NAME _____

☐ FREQUENT USER OF MANY SOFTWARE

   PACKAGES

☐ PROFESSIONAL PROGRAMMER

OTHER COMMENTS:

_____

_____

_____

_____

_____

_____

_____

PLEASE FOLD, SEAL, AND MAIL TO SYBEX

SYBEX, INC.
2021 CHALLENGER DR. #100
ALAMEDA, CALIFORNIA USA
           94501

SEAL